Perspectives on the Individual

UNIVERSITY CORE READINGS

Sixth Edition

Edited by

James Kuehl

Fairleigh Dickinson
University

Copley Custom Publishing Group
Acton, Massachusetts 01720

Acknowledgments:

pp. 8–17: Reprinted by permission of *The Sciences* from the March/April 1993 issue. Individual subscriptions are $21 per year. Write to: The Sciences, 2 East 63rd Street, New York, NY 10021.

pp. 19–38: From *Newsweek*, April 10, 2000. Copyright © 2000 by Newsweek, Inc. All rights reserved. Reprinted by permission.

pp. 39–44: From *Revised English Bible*. Copyright © 1989 by Oxford University Press and Cambridge University Press. Reprinted with permission.

pp. 45–48: From *Interbeing: Fourteen Guidelines for Engaged Buddhism*, Third Edition. Copyright © 1998 by Thich Nhat Hanh. Reprinted by permission of Parallax Press, Berkeley, California.

pp. 49–53: From *The Renaissance Philosophy of Man* edited by Ernst Cassirer, et al. Copyright © 1948 by University of Chicago Press. Reprinted by permission of the publisher.

pp. 66–68, 70–71: From *World Philosophy: A Text with Readings*, edited by Robert C. Solomon and Kathleen M. Higgins. Copyright © 1995. Published by McGraw-Hill, Inc.

pp. 68–70: From *Shobogenzo Zuimonki* by Dogen. Translated by Okumura Shohaku. Copyright © 1987 by Soto Zen Center, Kyoto.

pp. 72–74: From *The Unfettered Mind* by Takun Soho, translated by William Scott Wilson. Copyright © 1986 by Kondansha International, Tokoyo. Reprinted by permission.

pp. 75–119: "I Stand Here Ironing", copyright © 1956, 1957, 1960, 1961 by Tillie Olsen, "Tell Me a Riddle" from *Tell Me a Riddle* by Tillie Olsen. Introduction by John Leonard, copyright © 1956, 1957, 1960, 1961 by Tillie Olsen. Introduction 1994, Dell Publishing. Used by permission of Dell Publishing, A division of Random House, Inc.

Faculty

The readings in this book were selected by the faculty teaching Perspectives on the Individual.

Doris Auerbach, *Foreign Languages*

Thomas Beam, *Accounting*

John Becker, *English*

Joseph Billotti, *English*

Paul Boyer, *Geology*

Gary Bronson, *Information Systems*

Dawn Digrius, *History*

Louis DeBello, *Philosophy*

Mary Donovan, *English*

Deborah Fredericks, *English*

Cara Fuchs, *English*

Ellen Gerstle, *English*

Leonard Grob, *Philosophy*

William Hewson, *Art*

Maryann Hobbie, *Philosophy*

Francis Ingledew, *English*

Claude Jonnard, *Accounting*

Judith Kaufman, *Psychology*

Richard Kopp, *Foreign Languages*

Ron Kraus, *Psychology*

James Kuehl, *Philosophy*

Dorothy Mabey, *Mathematics*

Rendell Mabey, *Philosophy*

Odysseus Makridis, *Philosophy*

Elise Manganaro, *English*

Paula Mayhew, *English*

Peter Mullany, *English*

Edward Murray, *History*

June Price, *Nursing*

Elizabeth Pullen, *Sociology*

Ronald Roemer, *History*

Janet Stafford, *History*

Adele Stern, *Education*

Robert Vondienes-Oehm, *English*

Geoffrey Weinman, English

William Zander, *English*

CONTENTS

INTRODUCTION

All of us are involved in the process of becoming who we are as individual human beings. Whatever a person's particular situation, he or she is bound as a thinking person to reflect on who he or she is as an individual. Perspectives on the Individual asks you to reflect on the lives of interesting fictional and real persons. It asks you to think about these individuals in critical as well as personal ways. Thinking about the decisions of other individuals helps us understand our own personal decisions. Socrates wrestles with questions of personal integrity, Gilgamesh confronts the loss of his closest friend. Eva in "Tell Me a Riddle" raises serious questions about being in a family. Atwood* and Wiesel* give us a look at individuals placed in situations so extreme that the sanity and human quality of those persons almost disappear.

But the course is not simply devoted to the examination of individual encounters with significant situations. It also offers a look at the broader forces at work in a person's life. Freud* asks us to consider the emotional conflicts which consciously and unconsciously interfere with our quest for individual happiness. These conflicts stem from unacceptable urges of the unconscious. In contrast to Freud, the Buddhist offers a positive resource, no-mind, which although not self-conscious is not the essentially aggressive and egotistical unconscious of Freud. Wordsworth's turn toward Nature, Jesus' teaching on anger and hypocrisy, and Thich Naht Hanh's precepts on compassion challenge us to adjust radically our basic attitudes to the world and other people. The life of Malcolm X* illustrates how much attitudes and behavior patterns can change and the range of self-transformation which is possible. Pico della Miradola's optimism about the power of free will to transform the self almost seems confirmed.

* Margaret Atwood's *The Handmaid's Tale*, Elie Wiesel's *Night*, Sigmund Freud's *Civilization and Its Discontents*, and Alex Haley's *The Autobiography of Malcolm X* are required reading for the course in addition to the selections in this reader.

When we think of our individuality we often think of ways in which we are different from others. The course begins with a consideration of sexual differences among individuals. Our first reading, "The Five Sexes" challenges us to rethink distinctions which were perhaps over-simple. It also reminds us that the biological perspective is essential to any adequate understanding of the individual. The mapping of the human genome and developments in the study of genes and reproduction will undoubtedly lead to significant changes in our understanding of individuality and ourselves. One of these changes may result from a broader recognition of the extent to which we are genetically identical to each other and to other living creatures.

Specific objectives of the course include:

- facilitating the improvement of critical reasoning by talking and writing about important books,

- learning the importance of seeing problems in different contexts,

- relating issues, characters, and possible heroes to the problems we face now and will encounter in the future, and

- acquainting students with the major themes and issues of the texts which have been chosen by the faculty teaching Perspectives on the Individual.

Perspectives on the Individual treats central themes which come up in your other three Core courses. Cross Cultural Perspectives shows how cultures influence the ways individuals living in them think about themselves. The American Experience raises questions about individual rights and the quest for individual freedom in America. Global Issues and The Global Challenge detail the impacts that global problems have on individuals. Understanding oneself as part of the global setting is still a personal and individual adventure.

ARGUMENT AND OPINION IN THE UNIVERSITY CORE

John E. Becker

Respect

To some of you it may seem puzzling that professors in University Core courses ask you to give your own opinion, and then when you give it, they criticize it. After all, you have a right to your opinions. But as you know from experience, others feel they have a right to question your opinions. In the classroom professors have an *obligation* to do so. It's a vital aspect of the educational process. Questioning, in fact, is what all of us should do with all of our opinions. Critical thinking about your opinions is one of the aims, if not the primary aim, of the University Core curriculum. It is also one of the primary aims of university education. An uneducated person is a person who does not or cannot question her own opinions.

Your own behavior as students suggests that many of you already do a good deal of questioning of your ideas. Most professors are confronted daily with the reluctance of their students to express an opinion in class. Not all students are reluctant, but so many are that it constitutes one of the major problems of teaching. Why are students so reluctant to speak up? Many say it is because they are afraid they will say or ask something stupid. That is usually a false fear, but it is a very real feeling. And the ground of the fear is that you have questions not only about what you think but also about what you want to ask, and you would rather not be heard at all than be laughed at.

There is a way around this fear, but it may not be what you think: being fast on your feet, having lots of highly specialized information. No, you will lose this fear as you learn more positive ways to question what you think. Confidence in expressing your own opinion will arise as you learn to formulate your own ideas clearly, evaluate them, learn where you got them and the reasons you believe in them, and assess them in the light of what others think. You know about comparison shopping. You also know who your friends are. You can learn to judge ideas, too. As others begin to recognize that you have good reasons for what you think, that your opinions are thoughtful and based on solid information, they will treat your opinions with respect; and once you see that happen, confidence will come. It may sound like a paradox, but that confidence will last for as long as you continue to accept the possibility that you may be wrong. None of us ever escapes the need to question our own opinions.

So then, you have a right to your opinions, but the opinions themselves may not yet command much respect. If you want respect for your opinions, you will have to learn how to question them. The process is not simple. It may be slow and clumsy. And here another responsibility of your professors comes into play. It's their business to create an environment in which you won't feel what students too often feel: that their first halting steps toward expressing an informed opinion are stupid. Your opinions may not yet have the solidity that could win them respect outside the classroom. But even if *what* you say is not particularly impressive, you still have a right to respect as a person, especially if you are genuinely trying to state an opinion you have tried to think through carefully. A good teacher will never make fun of a student who is sincerely trying to understand herself, her friends, her inherited ideas and the new ones she is confronting every day in her university classes.

So we have two kinds of respect to keep clear, here. Everyone is owed a certain respect as a person, especially if she is a person who is trying to be thoughtful. The opinions of each of us, however, have a right only to as much respect as the opinions are worth.

A Way of Life

Learning how to question is not just acquiring a set of skills, for instance, better debating techniques. As a matter of fact, thinking critically may require a complete change in your style, not just of learning, but of living. The critical thinker is someone who makes a habit, a virtue, of looking for the truth of the matter, whatever it is, the human truth about individuals and groups, the scientific truth about the world we live in. As you may know from experience, and as you will certainly discover in your reading, people who are searching for the truth usually have to spend a good deal of time at it, pursuing one path, then being forced to abandon that path and look elsewhere. Eventually they discover some piece of the truth, and like the pearl of great price, they sell everything they have to purchase it. Important truths are rarely just a matter of getting a set of concepts all lined up. They are places we arrive at in our lives, moments in our life history, personal events.

But even when the critical thinker has arrived at some point of truth, she must remain open to new ideas and new ways of seeking out what may be more true or better. The critical thinker is never so sure of the truth of what she thinks that she can give up questioning. And so she questions not just her own opinions, but the opinions that are proposed to her by others, by her fellow students, by her professors.

Some of the truths we look for are personal and private. But often our convictions about the most private truths have repercussions for others, our families, our communities, even our country or the world. You have only to pick up a newspaper to discover a whole range of issues where private conviction reverberates far, issues such as abortion, environmental action, religious commitment. None of these questions manages to stay within the boundaries of our private and personal lives, and so our capacity to form thoughtful opinions about them is extremely important not just to ourselves but to society.

The search for the truth, then, is a central thread in the story of our lives. We look for it; we experiment and find ourselves mistaken; we look again, find it this time, and say, Yes, this is the truth. But then, something happens and we see that it was only a partial truth, and, like Malcolm X, we have to start off on another journey looking for a new truth that incorporates what we have discovered before and the new things we have learned. Our settling on the truth is always provisional, always open to new questions, as life opens up new possibilities that we hadn't appreciated before. Commitment with openness to change: that is the intellectual posture a mature person eventually arrives at.

Conceptual Truth, or Leaving It to the Experts

Some of the truths we are looking for tend to be expressed in rather abstract conceptual form: scientific truths, law, political philosophy, moral principles. You encounter many of these forms of thinking in university courses. You may even think that these are precisely the sorts of truths you come to a university to learn about, and you are partially right. Courses which deal in these sorts of concepts are usually concerned to convey to you an established body of thought, the conclusions that those who have developed the field have come to, conclusions which you must master before you can go on to do your own research, gather your own information, and form your own opinions. There is no getting around it, in a chemistry course you have to learn the periodic table, and at this point in your life nobody would be interested in hearing your opinion about it. Moreover, many of these courses train you to do a rather detached sort of critical thinking: you must understand the concepts, be able to follow the arguments, learn to assess the accuracy of the information on which the argument is based. These are often specialized skills peculiar to different fields, and no doubt many of you are eager to get into a field and learn the ideas and skills associated with it, since it appears that these are the tools you will need to get on with your life.

The truths taught in these areas, however, are never purely abstract, unrelated to personal lives, though they have abstract foundations. They are matters of expertise, and the danger is that you will too eagerly seek out your own area of expertise, dig yourself a nice hideout there, and leave matters that aren't in your field to others. We tend to be alienated by unfamiliar abstractions. We'd just as soon stay out of areas we haven't chosen to examine for ourselves. They seem to have little to do with our own lives—until some disaster strikes us, political, economic, or even physical, and we find we can't hide out in our field any longer.

The critical thinker respects expertise, but the critical thinker also knows, from his own experience if from nowhere else, the limits of expertise. Doctors know better than anyone that doctors don't know everything, and neither do lawyers, engineers, or politicians. There are situations when the facts are inconclusive to the expert, and then he has to lay them on the table before the layman and let him make the decision. This is most obvious in the area of medicine, but it is true in the largest areas of national and global policy. There are so many issues in so many fields that we all have to make decisions about, either directly, or by choosing to join an action group, or by voting. We simply have to have a basic capacity to do critical thinking in areas where we are not experts.

The problem with critical thinking in matters like this is not that it is too hard for the non-expert to do. You may not be able to understand everything about global warming, but you can always get more information, read a broad spectrum of opinions, check these out with your own experience and common sense, and come to at least a tentative conclusion. This is why University Core courses ask you to read Freud though you have no intention of becoming a psychologist, to read the Constitution and some amendments, though you have no intention of becoming a lawyer, to try to understand China and Africa, though you may never visit or do business there, and to get some idea of environmental problems and of the way science works in society, though you may be prejudiced, as many students are, against all forms of science. Without pretending to make you scientists or experts of any kind, University Core courses demonstrate the importance of applying your mind to many areas of common human concern. There's not very much we can afford simply to leave to the experts. You will face questions from different areas throughout your life, whether as a professional, an employee, or a voting citizen.

The Truths of Narrative

But the University Core asks you to do critical thinking about matters you should all be able to reflect on with genuine competence. Why do I say this? Though there are texts in the University Core that deal with matters of scientific or conceptual fact, many of them are narrative texts. Narratives require a different sort of critical thinking. They ask you to enter into sympathy with certain characters, to understand things from their point of view, to see the world through their eyes. What is critical thinking in this context? It is something quite familiar—or ought to be. It is the capacity to hold off from projecting your own feelings onto someone else, while at the same time using your own feelings to enter into their minds and imaginations.

You know, probably from hard experience, how disappointing your friends can be when you try to tell them about something and instead of listening carefully to you, they jump right in with an enthusiastic, "I know just what you mean!" and proceed to tell you about something completely different. So, one of the critical thinking skills you will have to learn is a very human one: skill at attending carefully to the story you are reading so that you are picking up precisely what the author is telling you about the characters in his narrative. Stories ask two things of you: (1) that you use your imagination to enter into the minds of the characters, and (2) that you restrain your imagination from projecting into the characters feelings and thoughts that the words of the story give you no grounds for finding there. You will probably find that frequently this is the area where your professor will criticize your opinions. She will ask you to go back to the text. Is what you have said grounded in the words of the text? Are you really getting what the character is suffering, or are you projecting your own vivid and urgent problems onto a story that is not really concerned with them?

What your professor is trying to teach you is a kind of critical thinking you might call "tact." Tact is the ability to sympathize without projecting, to listen carefully without intruding your own concerns. Tact is a supremely important skill to develop for all aspects of your life, not just for your university studies. Tact is not just a skill; it is one of the basic virtues of the humane person.

But there is more at stake here than training in personal relationships. You can acquire a very important kind of knowledge by developing tact. Many of our reactions, to people, to situations, to events, are determined by a set of short-hand concepts we carry around in our brains. Since we can't know everybody in the world around us as individuals, we create classifications of people. Sometimes these are just handy and harmless little rules of thumb that we are willing to toss aside once we get to know somebody better. But sometimes they are stereotypes—deeply rooted notions of what women are like, what men are like, what New Yorkers are like, what Californians, Frenchmen, Italians, Chinese, or Canadians are like. The trouble with these stereotypes is that they are often unconscious; we aren't aware that we are acting on them.

One of the reasons that you have been hearing and reading stories from your infancy, and that you will continue to read and think about them throughout your life, is that stories are our basic way of breaking out of stereotypes. We can never break out of them completely simply because we can never know everyone perfectly as individuals, but from the stories we read we get a larger and larger repertoire of human possibilities, of the many different ways people can think, can react, can imagine, can love, can face death. A man reading about a woman like Eva in Tillie Olsen's *Tell Me a Riddle*, may learn important things about the ways a woman thinks of motherhood. A student, reading the autobiography of Frederick Douglass, as you all will do in Core II, may discover something about what it was like to be a slave that her own experience would never have taught her.

And so there is much at stake in learning to read narratives carefully, to imagine their characters thoughtfully, making sure that you are understanding the character that is created by the words and not one that you would have created yourself if you were writing the story. To understand other people in their own individuality is to think critically about our own ways of categorizing the people of our world.

Conclusion

Critical thinking, then, is or ought to be the story of your life. You've always done some. In college you are challenged to do it more thoroughly and systematically. In the University Core you are encouraged to recognize that there are several different kinds of critical thinking and that there is hardly an area of your life in which critical thinking will not be necessary. You will, we hope, become expert in some field that will make you a success, but we also hope that you will become a careful and thoughtful person who brings to bear all the intellectual skills available to make sound critical judgments about people and things, science and society.

THE FIVE SEXES
WHY MALE AND FEMALE ARE NOT ENOUGH

Anne Fausto-Sterling

In 1843 Levi Suydam, a twenty-three-year-old resident of Salisbury, Connecticut, asked the town board of selectmen to validate his right to vote as a Whig in a hotly contested local election. The request raised a flurry of objections from the opposition party, for reasons that must be rare in the annals of American democracy: it was said that Suydam was more female than male and thus (some eighty years before suffrage was extended to women) could not be allowed to cast a ballot. To settle the dispute a physician, one William James Barry, was brought in to examine Suydam. And, presumably upon encountering a phallus, the good doctor declared the prospective voter male. With Suydam safely in their column the Whigs won the election by a majority of one.

Barry's diagnosis, however, turned out to be somewhat premature. Within a few days he discovered that, phallus notwithstanding, Suydam menstruated regularly and had a vaginal opening. Both his/her physique and his/her mental predispositions were more complex than was first suspected. S/he had narrow shoulders and broad hips and felt occasional sexual yearnings for women. Suydam's "feminine propensities, such as fondness for gay colors, for pieces of calico, comparing and placing them together, and an aversion for bodily labor, and an inability to perform the same, were remarked by many," Barry later wrote. It is not clear whether Suydam lost or retained the vote, or whether the election results were reversed.

Western culture is deeply committed to the idea that there are only two sexes. Even language refuses other possibilities; thus to write about Levi Suydam I have had to invent conventions—*s/he* and *his/her*—to denote someone who is clearly neither male nor female or who is perhaps both sexes at once. Legally, too, every adult is either man or woman, and the difference, of course, is not trivial. For Suydam it meant the franchise; today it means being available for, or exempt from, draft registration, as well as being subject, in various

8

ways, to a number of laws governing marriage, the family and human inti-
macy. In many parts of the United States, for instance, two people legally
registered as men cannot have sexual relations without violating anti-sodomy
statutes.

But if the state and the legal system have an interest in maintaining a two-
party sexual system, they are in defiance of nature. For biologically speaking,
there are many gradations running from female to male; and depending on
how one calls the shots, one can argue that along that spectrum lie at least five
sexes—and perhaps even more.

For some time medical investigators have recognized the concept of the
intersexual body. But the standard medical literature uses the term *intersex* as
a catch-all for three major subgroups with some mixture of male and female
characteristics: the so-called true hermaphrodites, whom I call herms, who
possess one testis and one ovary (the sperm- and egg-producing vessels, or
gonads); the male pseudohermaphrodites (the "merms"), who have testes and
some aspects of the female genitalia but no ovaries; and the female
pseudohermaphrodites (the "ferms"), who have ovaries and some aspects of
the male genitalia but lack testes. Each of those categories is in itself complex;
the percentage of male and female characteristics, for instance, can vary enormously among members of the same subgroup. Moreover, the inner lives of
the people in each subgroup—their special needs and their problems, attrac-
tions and repulsions—have gone unexplored by science. But on the basis of
what is known about them I suggest that the three intersexes, herm, merm
and ferm, deserve to be considered additional sexes each in its own right.
Indeed, I would argue further that sex is a vast, infinitely malleable continuum
that defies the constraints of even five categories.

Not surprisingly, it is extremely difficult to estimate the frequency of
intersexuality, much less the frequency of each of the three additional sexes: it is not the sort of information one volunteers on a job
application. The psychologist John Money of Johns Hopkins University, a
specialist in the study of congenital sexual-organ defects, suggests intersexuals
may constitute as many as 4 percent of births. As I point out to my students at
Brown University, in a student body of about 6,000 that fraction, if correct,
implies that there may be as many as 240 intersexuals on campus—surely
enough to form a minority caucus of some kind.

In reality though, few such students would make it as far as Brown in sexually diverse form. Recent advances in physiology and surgical technology now enable physicians to catch most intersexuals at the moment of birth. Almost at once such infants are entered into a program of hormonal and surgical management so that they can slip quietly into society as "normal" heterosexual males or females. I emphasize that the motive is in no way conspiratorial. The aims of the policy are genuinely humanitarian, reflecting the wish that people be able to "fit in" both physically and psychologically. In the medical community, however, the assumptions behind that wish—that there be only two sexes, that heterosexuality alone is normal, that there is one true model of psychological health—have gone virtually unexamined.

The word *hermaphrodite* comes from the Greek names Hermes, variously known as the messenger of the gods, the patron of music, the controller of dreams or the protector of livestock, and Aphrodite, the goddess of sexual love and beauty. According to Greek mythology, those two gods parented Hermaphroditus, who at age fifteen became half male and half female when his body fused with the body of a nymph he fell in love with. In some true hermaphrodites the testis and the ovary grow separately but bilaterally; in others they grow together within the same organ, forming an ovo-testis. Not infrequently, at least one of the gonads functions quite well, producing either sperm cells or eggs, as well as functional levels of the sex hormones—androgens or estrogens. Although in theory it might be possible for a true hermaphrodite to become both father and mother to a child, in practice the appropriate ducts and tubes are not configured so that egg and sperm can meet.

In contrast with the true hermaphrodites, the pseudohermaphrodites possess two gonads of the same kind along with the usual male (XY) or female (XX) chromosomal makeup. But their external genitalia and secondary sex characteristics do not match their chromosomes. Thus merms have testes and XY chromosomes, yet they also have a vagina and a clitoris, and at puberty they often develop breasts. They do not menstruate, however. Ferms have ovaries, two X chromosomes and sometimes a uterus, but they also have at least partly masculine external genitalia. Without medical intervention they can develop beards, deep voices and adult-size penises.

No classification scheme could more than suggest the variety of sexual anatomy encountered in clinical practice. In 1969, for example, two French investigators, Paul Guinet of the Endocrine Clinic in Lyons and Jacques Decourt of the Endocrine Clinic in Paris, described ninety-eight cases of true hermaphroditism—again, signifying people with both ovarian and testicular tissue—solely according to the appearance of the external genitalia and the accompanying ducts. In some cases the people exhibited strongly feminine development. They had separate openings for the vagina and the urethra, a cleft vulva defined by both the large and the small labia, or vaginal lips, and at puberty they developed breasts and usually began to menstruate. It was the oversize and sexually alert clitoris, which threatened sometimes at puberty to grow into a penis that usually impelled them to seek medical attention. Members of another group also had breasts and a feminine body type, and they menstruated. But their labia were at least partly fused, forming an incomplete scrotum. The phallus (here an embryological term for a structure that during usual development goes on to form either a clitoris or a penis) was between 1.5 and 2.8 inches long; nevertheless, they urinated through a urethra that opened into or near the vagina.

By far the most frequent form of true hermaphrodite encountered by Guinet and Decourt—55 percent—appeared to have a more masculine physique. In such people the urethra runs either through or near the phallus, which looks more like a penis than a clitoris. Any menstrual blood exits periodically during urination. But in spite of the relatively male appearance of the genitalia, breasts appear at puberty. It is possible that a sample larger than ninety-eight so-called true hermaphrodites would yield even more contrasts and subtleties. Suffice it to say that the varieties are so diverse that it is possible to know which parts are present and what is attached to what only after exploratory surgery.

The embryological origins of human hermaphrodites clearly fit what is known about male and female sexual development. The embryonic gonad generally chooses early in development to follow either a male or a female sexual pathway; for the ovo-testis, however, that choice is fudged. Similarly, the embryonic phallus most often ends up as a clitoris or a penis, but the existence of intermediate states comes as no surprise to the embryologist. There are also uro-genital swellings in the embryo that usually either stay open and become the vaginal labia or fuse and become a scrotum. In some hermaphrodites, though, the choice of opening or closing is ambivalent. Finally, all mammalian embryos have structures that can become the female uterus and the fallopian tubes, as well as structures that can become part of the male sperm-transport system. Typically either the male or the female set of those primordial genital organs degenerates, and the remaining structures achieve their sex-appropriate future. In hermaphrodites both sets of organs develop to varying degrees.

Intersexuality itself is old news. Hermaphrodites, for instance, are often featured in stories about human origins. Early biblical scholars believed Adam began life as a hermaphrodite and later divided into two people—a male and a female—after falling from grace. According to Plato there once were three sexes—male, female and hermaphrodite—but the third sex was lost with time.

Both the Talmud and the Tosefta, the Jewish books of law, list extensive regulations for people of mixed sex. The Tosefta expressly forbids hermaphrodites to inherit their fathers' estates (like daughters), to seclude themselves with women (like sons) or to shave (like men). When hermaphrodites menstruate they must be isolated from men (like women); they are disqualified from serving as witnesses or as priests (like women), but the laws of pederasty apply to them.

In Europe a pattern emerged by the end of the Middle Ages that, in a sense, has lasted to the present day: hermaphrodites were compelled to choose an established gender role and stick with it. The penalty for transgression was often death. Thus in the 1600s a Scottish hermaphrodite living as a woman was buried alive after impregnating his/her master's daughter.

For questions of inheritance, legitimacy, paternity, succession to title and eligibility for certain professions to be determined, modern Anglo-Saxon legal systems require that newborns be registered as either male or female. In the U.S. today sex determination is governed by state laws. Illinois permits adults to change the sex recorded on their birth certificates should a physician attest to having performed the appropriate surgery. The New York Academy of Medicine, on the other hand, has taken an opposite view. In spite of surgical alterations of the external genitalia, the academy argued in 1966, the chromosomal sex remains the same. By that measure, a person's wish to conceal his or her original sex cannot outweigh the public interest in protection against fraud.

During this century the medical community has completed what the legal world began—the complete erasure of any form of embodied sex that does not conform to a male-female, heterosexual pattern. Ironically, a more sophisticated knowledge of the complexity of sexual systems has led to the repression of such intricacy.

In 1937 the urologist Hugh H. Young of Johns Hopkins University published a volume titled *Genital Abnormalities, Hermaphroditism and Related Adrenal Diseases*. The book is remarkable for its erudition, scientific insight and open-mindedness. In it Young drew together a wealth of carefully documented case histories to demonstrate and study the medical treatment of such "accidents of birth." Young did not pass judgment on the people he studied, nor did he attempt to coerce into treatment those intersexuals who rejected that option. And he showed unusual even-handedness in referring to those people who had had sexual experiences as both men and women as "practicing hermaphrodites."

One of Young's more interesting cases was a hermaphrodite named Emma who had grown up as a female. Emma had both a penis-size clitoris and a vagina, which made it possible for him/her to have "normal" heterosexual sex with both men and women. As a teenager Emma had had sex with a number of girls to whom s/he was deeply attracted; but at the age of nineteen s/he had married a man. Unfortunately, he had given Emma little sexual pleasure (though *he* had had no complaints), and so throughout that marriage and subsequent ones Emma had kept girlfriends on the side. With some frequency s/he had pleasurable sex with them. Young describes his subject as appearing "to be quite content and even happy." In conversation Emma occasionally told him of his/her wish to be a man, a circumstance Young said would be relatively easy to bring about. But Emma's reply strikes a heroic blow for self-interest:

> Would you have to remove that vagina? I don't know about that because that's my meal ticket. If you did that, I would have to quit my husband and go to work, so I think I'll keep it and stay as I am. My husband supports me well, and even though I don't have any sexual pleasure with him, I do have lots with my girlfriends.

Yet even as Young was illuminating intersexuality with the light of scientific reason, he was beginning its suppression. For his book is also an extended treatise on the most modern surgical and hormonal methods of changing intersexuals into either males or females. Young may have differed from his successors in being less judgmental and controlling of the patients and their families, but he nonetheless supplied the foundation on which current intervention practices were built.

By 1969, when the English physicians Christopher J. Dewhurst and Ronald R. Gordon wrote *The Intersexual Disorders*, medical and surgical approaches to intersexuality had neared a state of rigid uniformity. It is hardly surprising that such a hardening of opinion took place in the era of the feminine mystique—of the post-Second World War flight to the suburbs and the strict division of family roles according to sex. That the medical consensus was not quite universal (or perhaps that it seemed poised to break apart again) can be gleaned from the near hysterical tone of Dewhurst and Gordon's book, which contrasts markedly with the calm reason of Young's founding work. Consider their opening description of an intersexual newborn:

> One can only attempt to imagine the anguish of the parents. That a newborn should have a deformity . . . [affecting] so fundamental an issue as the very sex of the child . . . is a tragic event which immediately conjures up visions of a hopeless psychological misfit doomed to live always as a sexual freak in loneliness and frustration.

Dewhurst and Gordon warned that such a miserable fate would, indeed, be a baby's lot should the case be improperly managed; "but fortunately," they wrote, "with correct management the outlook is infinitely better than the poor parents—emotionally stunned by the event—or indeed anyone without special knowledge could ever imagine."

Scientific dogma has held fast to the assumption that without medical care hermaphrodites are doomed to a life of misery. Yet there are few empirical studies to back up that assumption, and some of the same research gathered to build a case for medical treatment contradicts it. Francies Benton, another of Young's practicing hermaphrodites, "had not worried over his condition, did not wish to be changed, and was enjoying life." The same could be said of Emma, the opportunistic hausfrau. Even Dewhurst and Gordon, adamant about the psychological importance of treating intersexuals at the infant stage, acknowledged great success in "changing the sex" of older patients. They reported on twenty cases of children reclassified into a different sex after the supposedly critical age of eighteen months. They asserted that all the reclassifications were "successful," and they wondered then whether reregistration could be "recommended more readily than [had] been suggested so far."

The treatment of intersexuality in this century provides a clear example of what the French historian Michel Foucault has called biopower. The knowledge developed in biochemistry, embryology, endocrinology, psychology and surgery has enabled physicians to control the very sex of the human body. The multiple contradictions in that kind of power call for some scrutiny. On the one hand, the medical "management" of intersexuality certainly developed as part of an attempt to free people from perceived psychological pain (though whether the pain was the patient's, the parents' or the physician's is unclear). And if one accepts the assumption that in a sex-divided culture people can realize their greatest potential for happiness and productivity only if they are sure they belong to one of only two acknowledged sexes, modern medicine has been extremely successful.

On the other hand, the same medical accomplishments can be read not as progress but as a mode of discipline. Hermaphrodites have unruly bodies. They do not fall naturally into a binary classification; only a surgical shoehorn can put them there. But why should we care if a "woman," defined as one who has breasts, a vagina, a uterus and ovaries and who menstruates, also has a clitoris large enough to penetrate the vagina of another woman? Why should we care if there are people whose biological equipment enables them to have sex "naturally" with both men and women? The answers seem to lie in a cultural need to maintain clear distinctions between the sexes. Society mandates the control of intersexual bodies because they blur and bridge the great divide. Inasmuch as hermaphrodites literally embody both sexes, they challenge traditional beliefs about sexual difference: they possess the irritating ability to live sometimes as one sex and sometimes the other, and they raise the specter of homosexuality.

B ut what if things were altogether different? Imagine a world in which the same knowledge that has enabled medicine to intervene in the management of intersexual patients has been placed at the service of multiple sexualities. Imagine that the sexes have multiplied beyond currently imaginable limits. It would have to be a world of shared powers. Patient and physician, parent and child, male and female, heterosexual and homosexual—all those oppositions and others would have to be dissolved as sources of division. A new ethic of medical treatment would arise, one that might permit ambiguity in a culture that had overcome sexual division. The central mission of medical treatment would be to preserve life. Thus hermaphrodites would be concerned primarily not about whether they can conform to society, but about whether they might develop potentially life threatening conditions—hernias, gonadal tumors, salt imbalance caused by adrenal malfunction—that sometimes accompany hermaphroditic development. In my ideal world medical intervention for intersexuals would take place only rarely before the age of reason, subsequent treatment would be a cooperative venture between physician, patient and other advisers trained in issues of gender multiplicity.

I do not pretend that the transition to my utopia would be smooth. Sex, even the supposedly "normal," heterosexual kind, continues to cause untold anxieties in Western society. And certainly a culture that has yet to come to grips—religiously and, in some states, legally—with the ancient and relatively uncomplicated reality of homosexual love will not readily embrace intersexuality. No doubt the most troublesome arena by far would be the rearing of children. Parents, at least since the Victorian era, have fretted, sometimes to the point of outright denial, over the fact that their children are sexual beings.

All that and more amply explains why intersexual children are generally squeezed into one of the two prevailing sexual categories. But what would be the psychological consequences of taking the alternative road—raising children as unabashed intersexuals? On the surface that tack seems fraught with peril. What, for example, would happen to the intersexual child amid the unrelenting cruelty of the school yard? When the time came to shower in gym class, what horrors and humiliations would await the intersexual as his/her anatomy was displayed in all its nontraditional glory? In whose gym class would s/he register to begin with? What bathroom would s/he use? And how on earth would Mom and Dad help shepherd him/her through the mine field of puberty?

I n the past thirty years those questions have been ignored, as the scientific community has, with remarkable unanimity, avoided contemplating the alternative route of unimpeded intersexuality. But modern investigators tend to overlook a substantial body of case histories, most of them compiled between 1930 and 1960, before surgical intervention became rampant. Almost without exception, those reports describe children who grew up knowing they were intersexual (though they did not advertise it) and adjusted to their unusual status. Some of the studies are richly detailed—described at the level of gym-class showering (which most intersexuals avoided without incident); in any event, there is not a psychotic or a suicide in the lot.

Still, the nuances of socialization among intersexuals cry out for more sophisticated analysis. Clearly, before my vision of sexual multiplicity can be realized, the first openly intersexual children and their parents will have to be brave pioneers who will bear the brunt of society's growing pains. But in the long view—though it could take generations to achieve—the prize might be a society in which sexuality is something to be celebrated for its subtleties and not something to be feared or ridiculed.

Many of us hold the notion that science is objective, based on empirical evidence, and therefore, value free. The following readings on genetic research may provide a more skeptical point of view.

Genetic research is a development that will change the world as we know it in ways that we cannot foresee. It already effects our way of viewing ourselves in the universe. If we are 99.9% identical in our genetic structure, what makes us unique? If the genome is the essence of our being, what is the soul?

This scientific revolution holds the potential not only to fight disease and repair the body, but to challenge the inevitability of our own mortality. Yet "revolution" also means ungovernable and out of control. How will future generations be affected? Could we destroy the balance of the global ecosystem? Will only the wealthy and powerful benefit? What is the impact of knowing you carry a life threatening disease before a treatment or cure is available? Who will decide what defines a "good" gene? Do we need to weigh the benefits against the risks of creating a master race, of discriminating against the genetically "defective," or the formation of genetic structures that are alien and destructive to humanity?

These questions are threaded throughout the readings in Perspectives on the Individual. *In "The Five Sexes" we consider what is biologically "normal" and who should decide the question. Should we intervene in future generations?* The Handmaid's Tale *speaks to the consequences of the abuse of power, the genocide of the biologically inferior and the needs of society versus those of the individual. Socrates argued that the search for knowledge and justice is the ultimate good. In the 1400s, Pico della Mirandola postulated that humans have the innate capacity to equal or supercede the divine power of creation. Yet Freud and Wiesel spoke of our capacity for evil and degradation, and the struggle against our darker side.*

Good versus evil, control versus free will, and creation versus destruction are major themes in Perspectives on the Individual. *Can we/should we change the fundamental nature of humanity? As Christ counseled in "The Sermon on the Mount": "Beware false prophets. You will recognize them by their fruits."*

June Price

DECODING THE HUMAN BODY

Sharon Begley

Every Friday morning at 11, the directors of the five labs leading the race to decipher the human genome confer by phone to assess their progress. In mid-March, it was clear they were closing in on the next big milestone: reading the 2 billionth chemical "letter" in human DNA. But since some of those letters were redundant, a count of 2 billion would not really tell how close they were to the finish line of 3.2 billion.

Greg Schuler, a molecular biologist turned computer jock at the National Institutes of Health, had just spent the weekend, sitting on the sofa with his laptop in front of his fireplace at home, writing a 674-line program to reanalyze the overlaps. When he sicced it on the redundant sequences, the answer popped out: the Human Genome Project had *already* passed the 2 billion mark, on March 9. It had taken four years to determine the first billion letters in the human genome, but only four months for what Schuler calls "that next odometer moment." The actual chemical letter was—drumroll, please—T.

All right, so it didn't really matter which of the four letters making up DNA claimed position number 2,000,000,000 in the largest, most expensive, most ambitious biology project ever undertaken. But after 13 years and $250 million, through the work of some 1,100 biologists, computer scientists and technicians at 16 (mostly university) labs in 6 countries, the announcement meant that the Human Genome Project was two thirds of the way toward its goal of determining the exact chemical sequence that constitutes the DNA in every cell of every human body. With competitors in the private sector goading them on, scientists in the public project have tripled their pace, sequencing 12,000 letters every minute of every day, 24/7. By last weekend the project, financed by the U.S. government and Britain's Wellcome Trust, had sequenced 2,104,257,000 chemical letters. At this rate, it will complete its "working draft"— 90 percent of the genome, with an accuracy of 99.9 percent—in June. And science will know the blueprint of human life, the code of codes, the holy grail, the source code of *Homo sapiens*. It will know, Harvard University biologist Walter Gilbert says, "what it is to be human."

That knowledge promises to revolutionize medicine and vault the biotech industry into the Wall Street stratosphere. But just as no one foresaw eBay or Amazon when Apple unveiled the first home computer in 1977, so there is no crystal ball clear enough to reveal how knowing the entire human genome will change the way we live and even the way we think about who we are. It is a pretty good bet, though, that doctors will drip droplets of our genes onto a biochip to figure out if we have the kind of prostate cancer that will kill or not, or to figure out if ours is the kind of leukemia that responds to this drug rather than that one. They will analyze our children's genes to rank their chances of succumbing to heart disease or Alzheimer's. Scientists will learn which genes turn on when a wound heals, when a baby's fingers grow, when a scalp becomes bald or a brow wrinkled, when a song is learned or a memory formed, when hormones surge or stress overwhelms us—and they will learn how to manipulate those genes. Babies will be designed before conception. Employers will take your genetic profile before they offer you a job, or withdraw an offer if they don't like the cut of your DNA. The human genome sequence "will be the foundation of biology for decades, centuries or millennia to come," says John Sulston, director of the Sanger Centre, the genome lab near Cambridge, England, where a spiral staircase in the lobby twists upward like the double helix itself.

And all of it will emerge from something like this: ATGCCGCGGCTCCTCC . . . on and on, for about 3.2 billion such letters. Each letter represents a molecule—adenine, cytosine, guanine, thymine. Every cell of every human body, from skin to muscle to liver and everything in between (except red blood cells), contains a copy of the same DNA. The totality of DNA present in the cells of a species is its genome. Although the genetic age has brought incessant reports about genes "for" homosexuality, risk-taking, shyness, anxiety, cancer, Alzheimer's and more, the only thing a gene is actually "for" is a protein. The A's, T's, C's and G's constitute a code. Each triplet of letters instructs special machinery inside a cell to grab onto a particular amino acid. TGG, for instance, snatches the amino acid tryptophan. If you string together enough amino acids, you have a protein—a stomach enzyme that digests food, insulin that metabolizes carbohydrates, a brain chemical that causes depression, a sex hormone that triggers puberty. A gene, then, is an instruction, like the directions in a bead-making kit but written in molecule-ese. Humans have perhaps 80,000 genes, and we are 99.9 percent identical. That is, at only one in 1,000 chemical letters does the genome of, say, Woody Allen differ from that of Stone Cold Steve Austin.

Even at its inception, the creators of the Human Genome Project suspected that it would transform biology, vaulting it past physics as the hot science. But at the moment of its creation, the project was an unwanted child. Charles DeLisi, newly arrived at the Department of Energy, was in charge of research into the biological effects of radiation. In October 1985, he was reading a government report on technologies for detecting heritable mutations, such as those in the survivors of Hiroshima. It hit him: given the slow pace at which biologists were deciphering genes, which you need to do in order to assess mutations, they would finish . . . oh, about when humans had evolved into a new species. "We just weren't going to get there," says DeLisi. So he dashed off memos, ordered up reports, begged scientists to serve on planning committees—and got responses like "I don't want to spin my wheels" on a project that had little chance of happening.

For biologists and the genome, it was far from love at first sight. Critics pointed out that some 97 percent of the human genome—3.1 billion of the 3.2 billion A's, T's, C's and G's—does not spell out a gene. Why bother sequencing this "junk" DNA, whose presence no one can explain, especially when there was no known way to tell what was junk and what was a gene? But when a panel of leading scientists, including skeptics, unanimously endorsed the project in 1988, and it wrested funding from Congress, the Human Genome Project was out of the gate, headed toward a completion date of 2005 at a nice, sedate pace. It didn't last. In May 1998, gene-hunter extraordinaire J. Craig Venter and his newly formed Celera Genomics vowed to trounce the public project by finishing the human genome sequence in just three years. That made Francis Collins, director of the National Human Genome Research Institute, scramble. His labs had sequenced less than 3 percent of the genome at the original halfway point, so he ordered everyone to forget about the double-checking and the exploring of cool scientific puzzles and just churn out the *#@*ing A's, T's, C's and G's. It worked. In October 1998 Collins announced that his team would have a rough draft in 2001; in March 1999 he pushed it to this spring.

What will it mean to know the complete human genome? Eric Lander of MIT's Whitehead Institute compares it to the discovery of the periodic table of the elements in the late 1800s. "Genomics is now providing biology's periodic table," says Lander. "Scientists will know that every phenomenon must be explainable in terms of this measly list"—which will fit on a single CD-ROM. Already researchers are extracting DNA from patients, attaching fluorescent molecules and sprinkling the sample on a glass chip whose surface is speckled with 10,000 known genes. A laser reads the fluorescence, which indicates which of the known genes on the chip are in the mystery sample from the patient. In only the last few months such "gene-expression monitoring" has diagnosed a muscle tumor in a boy thought to have leukemia, and distinguished between two kinds of cancer that require very different chemotherapy. Soon, predicts Patrick Brown of Stanford University, expression analysis will distinguish prostate cancers that kill from prostate cancers that don't, neurons in a depressed brain from neurons in a normal brain—all on the basis of which genes are active.

Humankind's history is also written in its DNA. "Rare spelling differences in DNA can be used to trace human migrations," says Lander. "Scientists can recognize the descendants of chromosomes that ancient Phoenician traders left behind when they visited Italian seaports." Genetic data support the oral tradition that the Bantu-speaking Lemba of southern Africa are descendants of Jews who migrated from the Middle East 2,700 years ago. And they suggest that 98 percent of the Irish men of Connaught are descended from a single band of hunter-gatherers who reached the Emerald Isle more than 4,000 years ago.

But decoding the book of life poses daunting moral dilemmas. With knowledge of our genetic code will come the power to re-engineer the human species. Biologists will be able to use the genome as a parts list—much as customers scour a list of china to replace broken plates—and may well let prospective parents choose their unborn child's traits. Scientists have solid leads on genes for different temperaments, body builds, statures and cognitive abilities. And if anyone still believes that parents will recoil at playing God,

Locating Genes Within the Body . . .

The Human Genome Project is two-thirds completed. Scientists now know the exact identity of 2 billion chemical "letters" that make up human DNA.

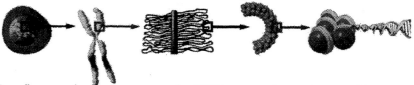

In a cell . . .   are chromosomes . . .   made of DNA   wrapped around   stretching to
                                          strands . . .   protein balls ...   five feet

and leave their baby's fate in the hands of nature, recall that couples have already created a frenzied market in eggs from Ivy League women.

Beyond the profound ethical issues are practical concerns. The easier it is to change ourselves and our children, the less society may tolerate those who do not, warns Lori Andrews of Kent College of Law. If genetic tests in utero predict mental dullness, obesity, short stature—or other undesirable traits of the moment—will society disparage children whose parents let them be born with those traits? Already, Andrews finds, some nurses and doctors blame parents for bringing into the world a child whose birth defect was diagnosable before delivery; how long will it be before the same condemnation applies to cosmetic imperfections? An even greater concern is that well-intentioned choices by millions of individual parents-to-be could add up to unforeseen consequences for all of humankind. It just so happens that some disease genes also confer resistance to disease: carrying a gene for sickle cell anemia, for instance, brings resistance to malaria. Are we smart enough, and wise enough, to know how knocking out "bad" genes will affect our evolution as a species?

From the inception of the genome project, ethicists warned that genetic knowledge would be used against people in insurance and employment. Sorting out whether this is happening is like judging whether HMOs provide quality care. Systematic surveys turn up few problems, but horror stories abound. One man underwent a genetic test and learned that he carried a marker for the blood disorder hemochromatosis. Although he was being successfully treated, his insurer dropped him on the ground that he might stop treatment and develop the disease. Another had a job offer withdrawn for "lying" during a pre-employment physical. He was healthy, but carried a gene for kidney disease. And last December Terri Seargent, 43, was fired from her

---

. . . Preparing for Study . . .

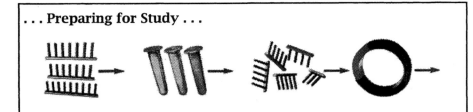

Shredding The DNA strand is cut into sections of 5,000 to 10,000 nucleotides

Freezing The DNA snippets are placed in vials and frozen for further analysis

Splicing The snippets are spliced into circular bacterial chromosomes

job as an office manager after she tested positive for the genetic disease that killed her brother. She began receiving preventive treatments. When her self-insured employer got the first bill, she was fired.

So far 39 states prohibit, at least in part, discrimination in health insurance based on genetic tests; 15 have some ban on discrimination in employment. But many of the laws have loopholes. (One of the 15 is North Carolina, where Seargent lives.) Employers still, apparently, want genetic information about their workers. A 1999 survey by the American Management Association found that 30 percent of large and midsize firms obtain such information on employees. Seven percent use it in hiring and promotions. "It is still possible to have information about your genome used to take away your health insurance or your job," says Collins. "As yet, we have not seen effective federal legislation [to prevent this]. With genes getting discovered right and left, the opportunities for mischief are on an exponential curve."

Perhaps the greatest unknown is how the completion of the Human Genome Project—not just getting C's, G's, T's and A's, but learning the function of every gene—will shape our views of what we are. There is a great risk of succumbing to a naive biological determinism, ascribing to our genes such qualities as personality, intelligence, even faith. Studies of twins have already claimed (to great criticism, but claimed nonetheless) that genes even shape whether an individual will favor or oppose capital punishment. "We do ascribe some sort of quasi-religious significance to our DNA," says Collins. "We have a tendency to be more deterministic than we should." For now, the power, and the limits, of the genome can only be guessed at. The stage is set. The players are ready. After millions of dollars and millions of hours, the curtain is rising on what our children will surely, looking back in awe, see as the dawn of the century of the genome.

... And Sequencing the Strands for Analysis

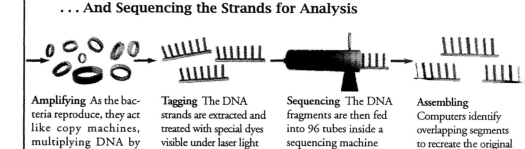

Amplifying As the bacteria reproduce, they act like copy machines, multiplying DNA by the billions

Tagging The DNA strands are extracted and treated with special dyes visible under laser light

Sequencing The DNA fragments are then fed into 96 tubes inside a sequencing machine

Assembling Computers identify overlapping segments to recreate the original nucleotide order

The Human Parts List

Scientists have identified more than 8,000 human genes, including those linked to breast and colon cancers and Alzheimer's disease. Figuring out how the genes work promises to lead to preventions and treatments. Some of the genes identified:

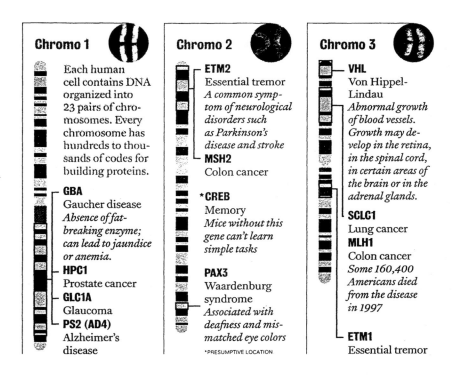

Chromo 1

Each human cell contains DNA organized into 23 pairs of chromosomes. Every chromosome has hundreds to thousands of codes for building proteins.

GBA
Gaucher disease
Absence of fat-breaking enzyme; can lead to jaundice or anemia.

HPC1
Prostate cancer

GLC1A
Glaucoma

PS2 (AD4)
Alzheimer's disease

Chromo 2

ETM2
Essential tremor
A common symptom of neurological disorders such as Parkinson's disease and stroke

MSH2
Colon cancer

*CREB
Memory
Mice without this gene can't learn simple tasks

PAX3
Waardenburg syndrome
Associated with deafness and mismatched eye colors

*PRESUMPTIVE LOCATION

Chromo 3

VHL
Von Hippel-Lindau
Abnormal growth of blood vessels. Growth may develop in the retina, in the spinal cord, in certain areas of the brain or in the adrenal glands.

SCLC1
Lung cancer

MLH1
Colon cancer
Some 160,400 Americans died from the disease in 1997

ETM1
Essential tremor

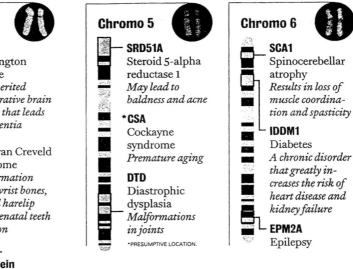

Chromo 4

HD
Huntington disease
An inherited degenerative brain disease that leads to dementia

EVC
Ellis-van Creveld syndrome
Malformation of the wrist bones, partial harelip and prenatal teeth eruption

Alpha-synuclein
Parkinson's disease
Only recently discovered to be hereditary

Chromo 5

SRD51A
Steroid 5-alpha reductase 1
May lead to baldness and acne

*CSA
Cockayne syndrome
Premature aging

DTD
Diastrophic dysplasia
Malformations in joints

*PRESUMPTIVE LOCATION.

Chromo 6

SCA1
Spinocerebellar atrophy
Results in loss of muscle coordination and spasticity

IDDM1
Diabetes
A chronic disorder that greatly increases the risk of heart disease and kidney failure

EPM2A
Epilepsy

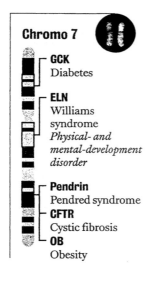

Chromo 7

GCK
Diabetes

ELN
Williams syndrome
Physical- and mental-development disorder

Pendrin
Pendred syndrome

CFTR
Cystic fibrosis

OB
Obesity

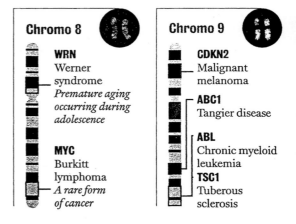

Chromo 8

WRN
Werner syndrome
Premature aging occurring during adolescence

MYC
Burkitt lymphoma
A rare form of cancer

Chromo 9

CDKN2
Malignant melanoma

ABC1
Tangier disease

ABL
Chronic myeloid leukemia

TSC1
Tuberous sclerosis

Chromo 10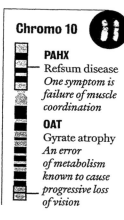

PAHX
Refsum disease
One symptom is failure of muscle coordination

OAT
Gyrate atrophy
An error of metabolism known to cause progressive loss of vision

Chromo 11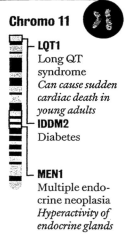

LQT1
Long QT syndrome
Can cause sudden cardiac death in young adults

IDDM2
Diabetes

MEN1
Multiple endocrine neoplasia
Hyperactivity of endocrine glands

Chromo 12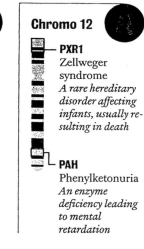

PXR1
Zellweger syndrome
A rare hereditary disorder affecting infants, usually resulting in death

PAH
Phenylketonuria
An enzyme deficiency leading to mental retardation

Chromo 13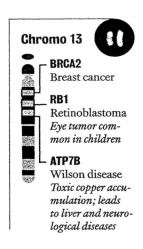

BRCA2
Breast cancer

RB1
Retinoblastoma
Eye tumor common in children

ATP7B
Wilson disease
Toxic copper accumulation; leads to liver and neurological diseases

Chromo 14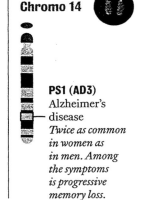

PS1 (AD3)
Alzheimer's disease
Twice as common in women as in men. Among the symptoms is progressive memory loss.

Chromo 15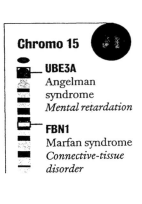

UBE3A
Angelman syndrome
Mental retardation

FBN1
Marfan syndrome
Connective-tissue disorder

Chromo 16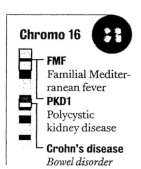

FMF
Familial Mediterranean fever

PKD1
Polycystic kidney disease

Crohn's disease
Bowel disorder

Chromo 17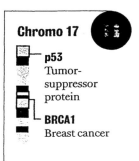

p53
Tumor-suppressor protein

BRCA1
Breast cancer

Chromo 18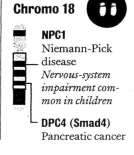

NPC1
Niemann-Pick disease
Nervous-system impairment common in children

DPC4 (Smad4)
Pancreatic cancer

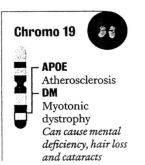

Chromo 19

- **APOE**
  Atherosclerosis
- **DM**
  Myotonic
  dystrophy
  *Can cause mental
  deficiency, hair loss
  and cataracts*

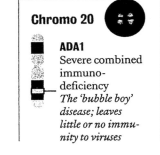

Chromo 20

- **ADA1**
  Severe combined
  immuno-
  deficiency
  *The 'bubble boy'
  disease; leaves
  little or no immu-
  nity to viruses*

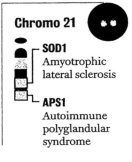

Chromo 21

- **SOD1**
  Amyotrophic
  lateral sclerosis
- **APS1**
  Autoimmune
  polyglandular
  syndrome

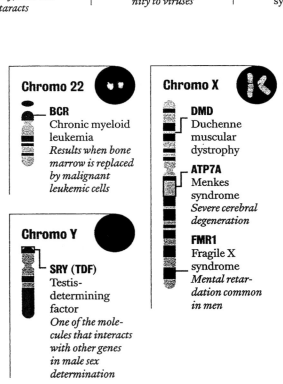

Chromo 22

- **BCR**
  Chronic myeloid
  leukemia
  *Results when bone
  marrow is replaced
  by malignant
  leukemic cells*

Chromo X

- **DMD**
  Duchenne
  muscular
  dystrophy
- **ATP7A**
  Menkes
  syndrome
  *Severe cerebral
  degeneration*
- **FMR1**
  Fragile X
  syndrome
  *Mental retar-
  dation common
  in men*

Chromo Y

- **SRY (TDF)**
  Testis-
  determining
  factor
  *One of the mole-
  cules that interacts
  with other genes
  in male sex
  determination*

A REVOLUTION IN MEDICINE

Geoffrey Cowley and Anne Underwood

Ann Miscoi had seen her father and her uncle die of organ failure in their mid-40s, so she figured she was lucky to be living when she turned 50 last year. The trouble was, she felt half dead. Her joints ached, her hair was falling out and she was plagued by unrelenting fatigue. Her doctor assured her that nothing was seriously wrong, even after a blood test revealed unusually high iron levels, but Miscoi wasn't so sure. Scanning the Internet, she learned about a hereditary condition called hemochromatosis, in which the body stores iron at dangerous concentrations in the blood, tissues and organs. Hemochromatosis is the nation's most common genetic illness, and probably the most underdiagnosed. As Miscoi read about it, everything started making sense—her symptoms, her blood readings, even her relatives' early deaths. So she found a doctor who would take her concerns more seriously.

Until recently, diagnosing the condition required a liver biopsy—not a procedure you'd undertake lightly. But Miscoi didn't have to go that route. Scientists isolated the gene for hemochromatosis a few years ago, and developed a test that can spot it in a drop of blood. Miscoi tested positive, and the diagnosis may well have saved her life. Through a regimen of weekly blood lettings, she was able to reduce her iron level before her organs sustained lasting damage. She's now free of symptoms, and as long as she gives blood every few months she should live a normal life span. "Without the DNA test," she says, "I would have had a hard time convincing any doctor that I had a real problem."

Hemochromatosis testing could save millions of lives in coming decades. And it's just one early hint of the changes that the sequencing of the human genome, now in its final stages, could bring. By 2010, says Dr. Francis Collins of the National Human Genome Research Institute, screening tests will enable anyone to gauge his or her unique health risks, down to the body's tolerance for cigarettes and cheeseburgers. Meanwhile, genetic discoveries will trigger a flood of new pharmaceuticals—drugs aimed at the causes of disease rather than the symptoms—and doctors will start prescribing different treatments for different patients, depending on their genetic profiles. The use of genes as medicine is probably farther off, but Collins believes even that will be routine within a few decades. "By 2050," he said recently, "many potential diseases will be cured at the molecular level before they arise."

That may be a bit optimistic, but the trends Collins foresees are already well in motion. Clinical labs now perform some 4 million genetic tests each year in the United States. Newborns are routinely checked for sickle cell anemia, congenital thyroid disease and phenylketonuria, a metabolic disorder that causes mental retardation. Like hemochromatosis, these conditions are catastrophic if they go undetected, but highly manageable when they're spotted early. Newer tests can help people from cancer-prone families determine whether they've inherited the culpable mutation. "My mother died of colon cancer at age 47," says Dr. Bert Vogelstein, an oncologist at Johns Hopkins and the Howard Hughes Medical Institute. "If we'd known she was [genetically] at risk, we could have screened for the disease and caught it early."

Early detection is just the beginning. Genes help determine not only whether we get sick but also how we respond to various treatments. "In the past," says Dr. William Evans of St. Jude Children's Research Hospital in Memphis, Tenn., "the questions were, 'How old are you and how much do you weigh?'" Now, thanks to recent genetic discoveries, physicians can sometimes determine who stands to benefit from a given drug, and who might be harmed by it. At St. Jude, doctors gauge the aggressiveness of children's leukemia cells before settling on chemotherapy or bone-marrow transplantation. And kids who qualify for chemo receive additional gene tests to gauge their tolerance. Most can handle standard doses of the drug mercaptopurine. But one person in 10 produces low levels of the enzyme needed to metabolize it, and for those folks a standard dose can be up to 20 times too high. By identifying those patients ahead of time, doctors can avoid poisoning them.

Cancer drugs aren't the only ones that vary in their effects. Experts estimate that 10 to 40 percent of the people taking any medication respond less than perfectly to it. The result is that 2 million Americans are hospitalized for adverse reactions each year, and 100,000 die. Only a handful of clinics are using gene tests to guide drug therapy, but the practice (known as pharmacogenetics) is spreading fast. Researchers are now learning to predict reactions to treatments for asthma, diabetes, heart disease and migraines—and firms like Incyte Genomics are developing chips that can analyze thousands of genes at a time. "My vision is that everyone will be sequenced at birth," says Dr. Mark Ratain of the University of Chicago. "Parents will get a CD-ROM with their child's genetic sequence. When physicians prescribe drugs, they'll use it to optimize treatment."

Unfortunately, knowledge is not always power. Knowing you're at extreme risk of breast cancer, or highly sensitive to a particular drug, may help you protect yourself. But suppose your family is plagued by Huntington's disease, or early-onset Alzheimer's. "There's nothing you can do about it if you test positive," says Nancy Wexler, a neuropsychologist at Columbia University. "You're not even spared of uncertainty, because you never know when the disease will start." Even testing *negative* for such a condition can complicate your life. Fifty-six-year-old Joyce Korevaar had spent years watching family members die of Huntington's when the first tests became available in the mid-1980s, so she was eager to know her own fate. Learning that she didn't have the mutation was like having a death sentence lifted. But the good news left her racked with guilt, and it distanced her from her less fortunate siblings. "Up until that point, we had all been in this together," she says. "Then I stepped out of the circle."

The hope, of course, is that we'll use genetic science to fix health problems, not just to predict them. After two decades of research, only a few gene-based therapies have entered clinical practice. But genetic science now informs every branch of medicine, from oncology to infectious disease, and it's opening countless possibilities. To paraphrase Francis Collins, we ain't seen nothing yet.

Classic gene therapy rests on a seductively simple idea. Since genes direct the assembly of every cell in the body, it should be possible to treat chronic health problems by slipping corrective genes into patients. Scientists have gotten good at isolating useful strands of DNA and splicing them into vehicles, or "vectors," that can penetrate cells. But getting the body to adopt and express therapeutic genes has been hellishly difficult. The most common vector—a genetically altered cold virus, or adenovirus—sets off an immune response that destroys the needed gene and can endanger the patient. When Jesse Gelsinger, a volunteer in a University of Pennsylvania gene-therapy experiment, died last year from adenovirus side effects, some experts demanded a halt to such trials. But newer vectors, such as "adeno-associated virus," are yielding better results with fewer side effects.

Even with the new vectors, gene therapy is at least a decade away from wide clinical use. But there are simpler ways to harness DNA. At Maryland-based Human Genome Sciences, for example, researchers are splicing human genes into bacterial cells that can be grown in culture. The cells then churn out proteins that can be given to patients as drugs. One of the company's products, known as MPIF-1, could help protect bone-marrow cells from the toxic effects of chemotherapy. Another protein, called KGF-2, may speed wound healing. These drugs are still in early clinical trials, but oncologists are already using similar agents to replenish immune cells decimated by chemotherapy.

While some teams race to harness useful genes, others are working to handcuff harmful ones. Genes, you'll recall, are functional segments of the long, double-stranded DNA molecules that make up chromosomes. They generate proteins by transcribing their codes onto single-stranded RNA molecules, which serve as templates for protein construction. The process begins when a so-called transcription factor grabs onto the gene's opening segment, or "promoter region," and crawls the length of the gene, generating an RNA molecule that carries the blueprint for a protein. Researchers have found that by flooding cells with fake copies of a gene's promoter region, they can divert transcription factors away from the actual gene, thus stalling the production of RNA. The technique has yet to reach the clinic, but that could happen soon. In one recent study, a team from Boston's Brigham and Women's Hospital found that decoy promoters slowed the buildup of scar tissue in veins used as bypass grafts. Veins doused with decoy promoters before surgery were less likely to become clogged.

If you can't keep a gene from making RNA, it's sometimes possible to keep the RNA from generating a harmful protein. The trick is to bombard it with tiny "antisense" molecules that block out parts of its sequence. And if that strategy fails, you can sometimes counter the protein itself. Consider the case of HER-2. It's a receptor protein that dots the surfaces of breast cells, enabling them to absorb growth signals. Most women have two copies of the gene for HER-2, but roughly a third of advanced breast-cancer patients have extra copies of the gene scattered about chromosome 17. As a result, their cells display up to 100 times the normal number of growth-signal receptors—not a winning feature when those cells happen to be malignant.

That was Ginger Empey's predicament five years ago. Her breast cancer had spread to her lymph nodes and liver by the time it was diagnosed, and conventional treatment did nothing for her. So the 50-year-old public-health nurse called UCLA from her home in Bakersfield, Calif., to see if she could join a clinical trial. As it happened, Dr. Dennis Slamon was testing a genetically engineered antibody called Herceptin, which blocks the HER-2 receptor. When tests showed that Empey's cells were swarming with the rogue protein, she was in. Her tumors shrank by a stunning 25 percent over the next year, so the researchers kept treating her. And after three and a half years of weekly injections, the tumors had essentially vanished. "My lesions were so small that the doctors couldn't tell whether they were cancer or scar tissue," she recalls.

Empey's lesions are still negligible after five years of treatment. Herceptin has made it to market, and researchers are now launching new studies to see how it affects patients with less-advanced disease. The drug is no panacea; most patients in the UCLA study responded for less than a year. But it stands as an emblem of how understanding the genome could advance the art of medicine. "Instead of building bigger bombs," says Slamon, "we've developed a smart bomb to target a specific problem." Let's hope that strategy prevails.

THE GOLD RUSH

Adam Bryant

C raig Venter, the president of Celera Genomics, loves to race. The brash scientist has competed, and won, in his 82-foot sailboat, called Sorcerer, which features a spinnaker with a 20-foot-tall image of a wizard—peaked hat and all—that bears a remarkable resemblance to its owner. Now he's applying that passion and drive to racing the government-funded Human Genome Project in a high-stakes contest to map the human body. To stay competitive in that race, his company is continually buying the latest, fastest computers. And given the run-up in his company's stock, he can more than afford to upgrade his personal toys as well. He's about to trade up to a 144-foot replica of an early New England schooner.

Forget Internet stocks. The race to commercialize the mysteries of the human genetic code has produced a stock-market bubble for the new millennium. Genomics has all the qualities that fast-moving, speculative money loves these days, including "Star Trek"-ian buzzwords like pharmacogenomics and bioinformatics. Investor chat rooms on the Internet are packed with biotech believers who adopt nicknames like Gene Wiz, Clone Head and Sequence Man. The fledgling industry also offers a lot more questions than answers, but these days investors call that "potential." And in this market, that means a license to ignore the relatively meager revenues and profits of many biotech companies and bid up their shares by more than 1,000 percent in a blink on the hope that maybe, just maybe, they might be the next Microsoft, Intel or Cisco.

The smart money is not just spreading bets on individual companies. Rival biotech firms are pursuing vastly different approaches to profiting from the basic research. There are, for example, the "pick and shovel" companies, an allusion to the fact that the only people who made real money during the gold rush were those who sold supplies to the miners. Those companies include PE Biosystems, which makes powerful devices that generate genomic data, and Affymetrix, which has developed a GeneChip system that analyzes gene sequences on disposable microchips.

Next are the software-service companies like Celera and Incyte. Their plans include selling databases of genetic information to drug companies and researchers, in much the same way that Bloomberg, for instance, sells customized financial data to brokerage houses and investors. Incyte already boasts about 25 subscribers, and many people are betting that Celera, which has harnessed tremendous computing power toward gene sequencing, will maintain an edge in this field.

Finally, there are companies like Human Genome Sciences and Millennium Pharmaceuticals that are trying to become giant drugmakers. They plan to use their in-house genetic research to develop medicines from scratch. Many of the established pharmaceutical players are believers, and have given these companies hundreds of millions of dollars in funding. Their potential is huge, given worldwide sales of successful drugs, but this is a business of long odds.

At this stage, perception is as important as reality, since the companies that look the most like winners will be rewarded with a high stock price, which they need to buy smaller rivals, lure talent and invest in costly new technology. So biotech executives are racing from TV appearances to photo shoots to radio and press interviews. These days the public-relations game is being won by Venter, president of Celera, and Dr. William A. Haseltine, chairman of Human Genome Sciences. Once colleagues in an earlier venture, they've gone their separate ways, even though their respective headquarters remain close to each other in Rockville, Md. (which is quickly becoming Genomics Junction). They may be scientists first, but they are equally adept promoters.

Venter relishes the role of the antiestablishment maverick—he barely graduated from high school, spent a lot of time surfing and was inspired to pursue science while doing medical triage work in Da Nang during the Vietnam War. He worked for the National Institutes of Health, and then helped set up the privately funded Institute for Genomic Research before setting sail with Celera. He's been compared in the media to Copernicus, Galileo, Newton and Einstein. He uses understatement to bolster the Venter Vision Thing. "My biggest worry," he says, "is that computing capacity won't grow fast enough to keep up with what our calculation needs are."

Haseltine, a fixture on the New York and D.C. social scenes, is more of an establishment player. He is also unwaveringly confident that Human Genome Sciences will simply add to his long list of scientific and business successes, which include leading-edge research on AIDS and starting a number of companies. He is already fixing his place in future history books. "The pharmaceutical industry has widely adopted a paradigm that I created," he says. "I take personal credit for catalyzing that change." He cultivates an image as a Renaissance man, choosing all the art works on the walls of the company's offices. The 1998 annual report is filled with images of 15th- and 16th-century paintings of ambassadors, noblemen and philosophers, with company officers striking similar poses on facing pages. A photo of Haseltine faces a full-page painting by Domenico Ghirlandaio of Saint Jerome, who was known not only for his ambition, hard work and famous library but also for his sometimes abrupt manner.

With the genomics industry still in its relative infancy, the business is driven by big claims as much as by science, and it can be tough keeping score. Celera trumpets that it has amassed DNA sequences covering 90 percent of the human genome. Haseltine says that he discovered virtually 95 percent of all genes more than four years ago. Incyte's CEO, Roy Whitfield, has said, "We have sequenced, patented and broadly licensed more genes than anyone else in this first critical phase of the genomics revolution." The executives regularly snipe at each other, too. Venter has called other scientists involved in sequencing the genome the "Liars' Club," because of the different ways they have calculated their costs and measured their achievements. Haseltine has often referred to Venter's bid to be the first to sequence the human genome as impractical, calling it "a race to nowhere, a race that shouldn't be run."

Some scientists are troubled by all the hyperbole. Maynard V. Olson, a professor of genetics at the University of Washington who has testified before Congress on the Human Genome Project, says he is concerned about the rise of "science by press release." The more traditional route, he believes, is for scientists to build on each other's work after it has been published in peer-reviewed journals.

It's easy to understand why the genome companies make such grand claims. After all, a full-grown commercial market for their products won't exist for years. Even Venter says it may take the next 100 years to completely understand all the data his company is generating this year. So people looking for quick cures will have to be patient. In the meantime, investors are eager for news, any news. As one biotech believer wrote recently in an Internet chatroom message, "Who knows when and what the next press release will reveal." These days, the fiercest race is to click the quickest on stock-trading accounts and join the genomics gold rush.

IT'S NOT 'ALL IN THE GENES'

Robert Sapolsky

I
t is no surprise that virtually every list that appeared of the most influential people of the 20th century included James Watson and Francis Crick, right up there alongside Churchill, Gandhi and Einstein. In discerning the double-helical nature of DNA, Watson and Crick paved the way for understanding the molecular biology of the gene, the dominant scientific accomplishment of the postwar era. Sequencing the human genome will represent a closure of sorts for the revolution wrought by those two geniuses.

At the same time, it's also not surprising that many people get nervous at the prospects of that scientific milestone. It will no doubt be a revolution, but there are some scary "Brave New World" overtones that raise fundamental questions about how we will think about ourselves. Will it mean that our behaviors, thoughts and emotions are merely the sum of our genes, and scientists can use a genetic roadmap to calculate just what that sum is? Who are we then, and what will happen to our cherished senses of individuality and free will? Will knowing our genetic code mean we will know our irrevocable fates?

I don't share that fear, and let me explain why. At the crux of the anxiety is the notion of the Primacy of Genes. This is the idea that if you want to explain some big, complex problem in biology (like why some particular bird migrates south for the winter, or why a particular person becomes schizophrenic), the answer lies in understanding the building blocks that make up those phenomena—and that those building blocks are ultimately genes. In this deterministic view, the proteins unleashed by genes "cause" or "control" behavior. Have the wrong version of a gene and, bam, you're guaranteed something awful, like being pathologically aggressive, or having schizophrenia. Everything is preordained from conception.

Yet hardly any genes actually work this way. Instead, genes and environment interact; nurture reinforces or retards nature. For example, research indicates that "having the gene for schizophrenia" means there is a 50 percent risk you'll develop the disease, rather than absolute certainty. The disease occurs only when you have a combination of schizophrenia-prone genes and schizophrenia-inducing experiences. A particular gene can have a different effect, depending on the environment. There is genetic vulnerability, but not inevitability.

The Primacy of Genes also assumes that genes act on their own. How do they know when to turn on and off the synthesis of particular proteins? If you view genes as autonomous, the answer is that they just know. No one tells a gene what to do; instead, the buck starts and stops there.

However, that view is far from accurate too. Within the staggeringly long sequences of DNA, it turns out that only a tiny percentage of letters actually form the words that constitute genes and serve as code for proteins. More than 95 percent of DNA, instead, is "non-coding." Much of DNA simply constitutes on and off switches for regulating the activity of genes. It's like you have a 100-page book, and 95 of the pages are instructions and advice for reading the other five pages. Thus, genes don't independently determine when proteins are synthesized. They follow instructions originating somewhere else.

What regulates those switches? In some instances, chemical messengers from other parts of the cell. In other cases, messengers from other cells in the body (this is the way many hormones work). And, critically, in still other cases, genes are turned on or off by environmental factors. As a crude example, some carcinogens work by getting into cells, binding to one of those DNA switches and turning on genes that cause the uncontrolled growth that constitutes cancer. Or a mother rat licking and grooming her infant will initiate a cascade of events that eventually turns on genes related to growth in that child. Or the smell of a female in heat will activate genes in certain male primates related to reproduction. Or a miserably stressful day of final exams will activate genes in a typical college student that will suppress the immune system, often leading to a cold or worse.

You can't dissociate genes from the environment that turns genes on and off. And you can't dissociate the effects of genes from the environment in which proteins exert their effects. The study of genetics will never be so all encompassing as to gobble up every subject from medicine to sociology. Instead, the more science learns about genes, the more we will learn about the importance of the environment. That goes for real life, too: genes are essential but not the whole story.

from THE SERMON ON THE MOUNT

The Gospel of Matthew

5

When he saw the crowds he went up a mountain. There he sat down, and when his disciples had gathered round him he began to address them. And this is the teaching he gave:

> Blessed are the poor in spirit;
> the kingdom of Heaven is theirs.
> Blessed are the sorrowful;
> they shall find consolation.
> Blessed are the gentle;
> they shall have the earth for their possession.
> Blessed are those who hunger and thirst to see right prevail;
> they shall be satisfied.
> Blessed are those who show mercy;
> mercy shall be shown to them.
> Blessed are those whose hearts are pure;
> they shall see God.
> Blessed are the peacemakers;
> they shall be called God's children.
> Blessed are those who are persecuted in the cause of right;
> the kingdom of Heaven is theirs.

Blessed are you, when you suffer insults and persecution and calumnies of every kind for my sake. Exult and be glad, for you have a rich reward in heaven; in the same way they persecuted the prophets before you.

You are salt to the world. And if salt becomes tasteless, how is its saltness to be restored? It is good for nothing but to be thrown away and trodden underfoot.

You are light for all the world. A town that stands on a hill cannot be hidden. When a lamp is lit, it is not put under the meal-tub, but on a lampstand, where it gives light to everyone in the house. Like the lamp, you must shed light among your fellows, so that, when they see the good you do, they may give praise to your Father in heaven.

Do not suppose that I have come to abolish the law and the prophets; I did not come to abolish, but to complete. Truly I tell you: so long as heaven and earth endure, not a letter, not a dot, will disappear from the law until all that must happen has happened. Anyone therefore who sets aside even the least of the law's demands, and teaches others to do the same, will have the lowest place in the kingdom of Heaven, whereas anyone who keeps the law, and teaches others to do so, will rank high in the kingdom of Heaven. I tell you, unless you show yourselves far better than the scribes and Pharisees, you can never enter the kingdom of Heaven.

You have heard that our forefathers were told, "Do not commit murder; anyone who commits murder must be brought to justice." But what I tell you is this: Anyone who nurses anger against his brother must be brought to justice. Whoever calls his brother "good for nothing" deserves the sentence of the court; whoever calls him "fool" deserves hell-fire. So if you are presenting your gift at the altar and suddenly remember that your brother has a grievance against you, leave your gift where it is before the altar. First go and make your peace with your brother; then come back and offer your gift. If someone sues you, come to terms with him promptly while you are both on your way to court; otherwise he may hand you over to the judge, and the judge to the officer, and you will be thrown into jail. Truly I tell you: once you are there you will not be let out until you have paid the last penny.

You have heard that they were told, "do not commit adultery." But what I tell you is this: If a man looks at a woman with a lustful eye, he has already committed adultery with her in his heart. If your right eye causes your downfall, tear it out and fling it away; it is better for you to lose one part of your body than for the whole of it to be thrown into hell. If your right hand causes your downfall, cut if off and fling it away; it is better for you to lose one part of your body than for the whole of it to go to hell.

They were told, "A man who divorces his wife must give her a certificate of dismissal." But what I tell you is this: If a man divorces his wife for any cause other than unchastity he involves her in adultery; and whoever marries her commits adultery.

Again, you have heard that our forefathers were told, "Do not break your oath," and, "Oaths sworn to the Lord must be kept." But what I tell you is this: You are not to swear at all—not by heaven, for it is God's throne, nor by the earth, for it is his footstool, nor by Jerusalem, for it is the city of the great

King, nor by your own head, because you cannot turn one hair of it white or black. Plain "Yes" or "No" is all you need to say; anything beyond that comes from the evil one.

You have heard that they were told, "An eye for an eye, a tooth for a tooth." But what I tell you is this: Do not resist those who wrong you. If anyone slaps you on the right cheek, turn and offer him the other also. If anyone wants to sue you and takes your shirt, let him have your cloak as well. If someone in authority presses you into service for one mile, go with him two. Give to anyone who asks; and do not turn your back on anyone who wants to borrow.

You have heard that they were told, "Love your neighbour and hate your enemy." But what I tell you is this: Love your enemies and pray for your persecutors; only so can you be children of your heavenly Father, who causes the sun to rise on good and bad alike, and sends the rain on the innocent and the wicked. If you love only those who love you, what reward can you expect? Even the tax-collectors do as much as that. If you greet only your brothers, what is there extraordinary about that? Even the heathen do as much. There must be no limit to your goodness, as your heavenly Father's goodness knows no bounds.

6

Be careful not to parade your religion before others; if you do, no reward awaits you with your Father in heaven.

So when you give alms do not announce it with a flourish of trumpets, as the hypocrites do in synagogues and in the streets to win the praise of others. Truly I tell you: they have their reward already. But when you give alms, do not let your left hand know what your right is doing; your good deed must be secret, and your Father who sees what is done in secret will reward you.

Again when you pray, do not be like the hypocrites; they love to say their prayers standing up in synagogues and at street corners for everyone to see them. Truly I tell you: they have their reward already. But when you pray, go into a room by yourself, shut the door, and pray to your Father who is in secret; and your Father who sees what is done in secret will reward you.

In your prayers do not go babbling on like the heathen, who imagine that the more they say the more likely they are to be heard. Do not imitate them, for your Father knows what your needs are before you ask him.

This is how you should pray:

Our Father in heaven.
may your name be hallowed;
your kingdom come,
your will be done,
on earth as in heaven.
Give us today our daily bread.
Forgive us the wrong we have done,
as we have forgiven those who have wronged us.
And do not put us to the test,
but save us from the evil one.

For if you forgive others the wrongs they have done, your heavenly Father will also forgive you; but if you do not forgive others, then your Father will not forgive the wrongs that you have done.

So too when you fast, do not look gloomy like the hypocrites: they make their faces unsightly so that everybody may see that they are fasting. Truly I tell you: they have their reward already. But when you fast, anoint your head and wash your face, so that no one sees that you are fasting, but only your Father who is in secret; and your Father who sees what is done in secret will give you your reward.

Do not store up for yourselves treasure on earth, where moth and rust destroy, and thieves break in and steal; but store up treasure in heaven, where neither moth nor rust will destroy, nor thieves break in and steal. For where your treasure is, there will your heart be also.

The lamp of the body is the eye. If your eyes are sound, you will have light for your whole body; if your eyes are bad, your whole body will be in darkness. If then the only light you have is darkness, how great a darkness that will be.

No one can serve two masters; for either he will hate the first and love the second, or he will be devoted to the first and despise the second. You cannot serve God and Money.

This is why I tell you not to be anxious about food and drink to keep you alive and about clothes to cover your body. Surely life is more than food, the body more than clothes. Look at the birds in the sky; they do not sow and reap and store in barns, yet your heavenly Father feeds them. Are you not worth more than the birds? Can anxious thought add a single day to your life? And why be anxious about clothes? Consider how the lilies grow in the fields; they do not work, they do not spin; yet I tell you, even Solomon in all his splendour was not attired like one of them. If that is how God clothes the grass in the fields, which is there today and tomorrow is thrown on the stove, will he not all the more clothe you? How little faith you have! Do not ask anxiously, "What are we to eat? What are we to drink? What shall we wear?" These are the things that occupy the minds of the heathen, but your heavenly Father knows that you need them all. Set your mind on God's kingdom and his justice before everything else, and all the rest will come to you as well. So do not be anxious about tomorrow; tomorrow will look after itself. Each day has troubles enough of its own.

7

Do not judge, and you will not be judged. For as you judge others, so you will yourselves be judged, and whatever measure you deal out to others will be dealt to you. Why do you look at the speck of sawdust in your brother's eye, with never a thought for the plank in your own? How can you say to your brother, "Let me take the speck out of your eye," when all the time there is a plank in your own? You hypocrite! First take the plant out of your own eye, and then you will see clearly to take the speck out of your brother's.

Do not give dogs what is holy; do not throw your pearls to the pigs: they will only trample on them, and turn and tear you to pieces.

Ask, and you will receive; seek, and you will find; knock, and the door will be opened to you. For everyone who asks receives, those who seek find, and to those who knock, the door will be opened.

Would any of you offer his son a stone when he asks for bread, or a snake when he asks for a fish? If you, bad as you are, know how to give good things to your children, how much more will your heavenly Father give good things to those who ask him!

Always treat others as you would like them to treat you: that is the law and the prophets.

Enter by the narrow gate. Wide is the gate and broad the road that leads to destruction, and many enter that way; narrow is the gate and constricted the road that leads to life, and those who find them are few.

Beware of false prophets, who come to you dressed up as sheep while underneath they are savage wolves. You will recognize them by their fruit. Can grapes be picked from briars, or figs from thistles? A good tree always yields sound fruit, and a poor tree bad fruit. A good tree cannot bear bad fruit, or a poor tree sound fruit. A tree that does not yield sound fruit is cut down and thrown on the fire. That is why I say you will recognize them by their fruit.

Not everyone who says to me, "Lord, Lord" will enter the kingdom of Heaven, but only those who do the will of my heavenly Father. When the day comes, many will say to me, "Lord, Lord, did we not prophesy in your name, drive out demons in your name, and in your name perform many miracles?" Then I will tell them plainly, "I never knew you. Out of my sight; your deeds are evil!"

So whoever hears these words of mine and acts on them is like a man who had the sense to build his house on rock. The rain came down, the floods rose, the winds blew and beat upon that house; but it did not fall, because its foundations were on rock. And whoever hears these words of mine and does not act on them is like a man who was foolish enough to build his house on sand. The rain came down, the floods rose, the winds blew and battered against that house; and it fell with a great crash.

When Jesus had finished this discourse the people were amazed at his teaching; unlike their scribes he taught with a note of authority.

In the midst of the Vietnam war, Thich Nhat Hanh, a Buddhist monk, formed a small group, the Order of Interbeing (Tiep Hien), to promote peacefulness and reconciliation. The group's Fourteen Mindfulness Trainings *are meant as a guide to engaged compassionate living, recognizing and responding to the suffering of all living beings. The idea of "mindfulness" is close to the idea of "understanding" in both the sense of having understanding and the sense of being understanding. It also means being awake, here and now, and having a calm and peaceful mind.*

Rendell Mabey

THE FOURTEEN MINDFULNESS TRAININGS

Thich Nhat Hanh

1

Aware of the suffering created by fanaticism and intolerance, we are determined not to be idolatrous about or bound to any doctrine, theory, or ideology, even Buddhist ones. Buddhist teachings are guiding means to help us learn to look deeply and to develop our understanding and compassion. They are not doctrines to fight, kill, or die for.

2

Aware of the suffering created by attachment to views and wrong perceptions, we are determined to avoid being narrow-minded and bound to present views. We shall learn and practice nonattachment from views in order to be open to others' insights and experiences. We are aware that the knowledge we presently possess is not changeless, absolute truth. Truth is found in life, and we will observe life within and around us in every moment, ready to learn throughout our lives.

3

Aware of the suffering brought about when we impose our views on others, we are committed not to force others, even our children, by any means whatsoever—such as authority, threat, money, propaganda, or indoctrination—to adopt our views. We will respect the right of others to be different and to choose what to believe and how to decide. We will, however, help others renounce fanaticism and narrowness through practicing deeply and engaging in compassionate dialogue.

4

Aware that looking deeply at the nature of suffering can help us develop compassion and find ways out of suffering, we are determined not to avoid or close our eyes before suffering. We are committed to finding ways, including personal contact, images, and sounds, to be with those who suffer, so we can understand their situation deeply and help them transform their suffering into compassion, peace, and joy.

5

Aware that true happiness is rooted in peace, solidity, freedom, and compassion, and not in wealth or fame, we are determined not to take as the aim of our life fame, profit, wealth, or sensual pleasure, nor to accumulate wealth while millions are hungry and dying. We are committed to living simply and sharing our time, energy, and material resources with those in need. We will practice mindful consuming, not using alcohol, drugs, or any other products that bring toxins into our own and the collective body and consciousness.

6

Aware that anger blocks communication and creates suffering, we are determined to take care of the energy of anger when it arises and to recognize and transform the seeds of anger that lie deep in our consciousness. When anger comes up, we are determined not to do or say anything, but to practice mindful breathing or mindful walking and acknowledge, embrace, and look deeply into our anger. We will learn to look with the eyes of compassion at ourselves and at those we think are the cause of our anger.

7

Aware that life is available only in the present moment and that it is possible to live happily in the here and now, we are committed to training ourselves to live deeply each moment of daily life. We will try not to lose ourselves in dispersion or be carried away by regrets about the past, worries about the future, or craving, anger, or jealousy in the present. We will practice mindful breathing to come back to what is happening in the present moment. We are determined to learn the art of mindful living by touching the wondrous, refreshing, and healing elements that are inside and around us, and by nourishing seeds of joy, peace, love, and understanding in ourselves, thus facilitating the work of transformation and healing in our consciousness.

8

Aware that lack of communication always brings separation and suffering, we are committed to training ourselves in the practice of compassionate listening and loving speech. We will learn to listen deeply without judging or reacting and refrain from uttering words that can create discord or cause the community to break. We will make every effort to keep communications open and to reconcile and resolve all conflicts, however small.

9

Aware that words can create suffering or happiness, we are committed to learning to speak truthfully and constructively, using only words that inspire hope and confidence. We are determined not to say untruthful things for the sake of personal interest or to impress people, nor to utter words that might cause division or hatred. We will not spread news that we do not know to be certain nor criticize or condemn things of which we are not sure. We will do our best to speak out about situations of injustice, even when doing so may threaten our safety.

10

Aware that the essence and aim of a Sangha is the practice of understanding and compassion, we are determined not to use the Buddhist community for personal gain or profit or transform our community into a political instrument. A spiritual community should, however, take a clear stand against oppression and injustice and should strive to change the situation without engaging in partisan conflicts.

11

Aware that great violence and injustice have been done to our environment and society, we are committed not to live with a vocation that is harmful to humans and nature. We will do our best to select a livelihood that helps realize our ideal of understanding and compassion. Aware of global economic, political and social realities, we will behave responsibly as consumers and as citizens, not supporting companies that deprive others of their chance to live.

12

Aware that much suffering is caused by war and conflict, we are determined to cultivate nonviolence, understanding, and compassion in our daily lives, to promote peace education, mindful mediation, and reconciliation within families, communities, nations, and in the world. We are determined not to kill and not to let others kill. We will diligently practice deep looking with our Sangha to discover better ways to protect life and prevent war.

13

Aware of the suffering caused by exploitation, social injustice, stealing, and oppression, we are committed to cultivating loving kindness and learning ways to work for the well-being of people, animals, plants, and minerals. We will practice generosity by sharing our time, energy, and material resources with those who are in need. We are determined not to steal and not to possess anything that should belong to others. We will respect the property of others, but will try to prevent others from profiting from human suffering or the suffering of other beings.

14

(For lay members): Aware that sexual relations motivated by craving cannot dissipate the feeling of loneliness but will create more suffering, frustration, and isolation, we are determined not to engage in sexual relations without mutual understanding, love, and a long-term commitment. In sexual relations, we must be aware of future suffering that may be caused. We know that to preserve the happiness of ourselves and others, we must respect the rights and commitments of ourselves and others. We will do everything in our power to protect children from sexual abuse and to protect couples and families from being broken by sexual misconduct. We will treat our bodies with respect and preserve our vital energies (sexual, breath, spirit) for the realization of our bodhisattva ideal. We will be fully aware of the responsibility of bringing new lives into the world, and will meditate on the world into which we are bringing new beings.

(For monastic members): Aware that the aspiration of a monk or a nun can only be realized when he or she wholly leaves behind the bonds of worldly love, we are committed to practicing chastity and to helping others protect themselves. We are aware that loneliness and suffering cannot be alleviated by the coming together of two bodies in a sexual relationship, but by the practice of true understanding and compassion. We know that a sexual relationship will destroy our life as a monk or a nun, will prevent us from realizing our ideal of serving living beings, and will harm others. We are determined not to suppress or mistreat our body or to look upon our body as only an instrument, but to learn to handle our body with respect. We are determined to preserve vital energies (sexual, breath, spirit) for the realization of our bodhisattva ideal.

Giovanni Pico, Earl of Mirandola, Italy, was born in 1463. He lived to be only 31. By the time he was 25 he had been arrested in Lyons, France, because of his philosophical controversies with Pope Innocent VIII. His attempt to bring Plato's ideas into harmony with Christianity led to conflict with religious authority In the reading which follows you will note that Pico links Moses with a work of Plato called the Timaeus. *Pico's central idea in the reading is revolutionary and disquieting. Do you agree with it? It has profoundly influenced our civilization.*

ORATION ON THE DIGNITY OF MAN

Pico della Mirandola

"There is nothing to be seen more wonderful than man." In agreement with this opinion is the saying of Hermes Trismegistus: "A great miracle, Asclepius, is man." But when I weighed the reason for these maxims, the many grounds for the excellence of human nature reported by many men failed to satisfy me—that man is the intermediary between creatures, the intimate of the gods, the king of the lower beings, by the acuteness of his senses, by the discernment of his reason, and by the light of his intelligence the interpreter of nature, the interval between fixed eternity and fleeting time, and (as the Persians say) the bond, nay, rather, the marriage song of the world, on David's testimony but little lower than the angels. Admittedly great though these reasons be, they are not the principal grounds, that is, those which may rightfully claim for themselves the privilege of the highest admiration. For why should we not admire more the angels themselves and the blessed choirs of heaven? At last it seems to me I have come to understand why man is the most fortunate of creatures and consequently worthy of all admiration and what precisely is that rank which is his lot in the universal chain of Being—a rank to be envied not only by brutes but even by the stars and by minds beyond this world. It is a matter past faith and a wondrous one. Why should it not be? For it is on this very account that man is rightly called and judged a great miracle and a wonderful creature indeed.

2. But hear, Fathers, exactly what this rank is and, as friendly auditors, conformably to your kindness, do me this favor. God the Father, the supreme Architect, had already built this cosmic home we behold, the most sacred

temple of His godhead, by the laws of his mysterious wisdom. The region above the heavens He had adorned with Intelligences, the heavenly spheres He had quickened with eternal souls, and the excrementary and filthy parts of the lower world He had filled with a multitude of animals of every kind. But when the work was finished, the Craftsman kept wishing that there were someone to ponder the plan of so great a work, to love its beauty, and to wonder at its vastness. Therefore, when everything was done (as Moses and Timaeus bear witness) He finally took thought concerning the creation of man. But there was not among His archetypes that from which He could fashion a new offspring, nor was there in his treasure houses anything which He might bestow on His new son as an inheritance, nor was there in the seats of all the world a place where the latter might sit to contemplate the universe. All was now complete; all things had been assigned to the highest, the middle, and the lowest orders. But in its final creation it was not the part of the Father's power to fail as though exhausted. It was not the part of His wisdom to waver in a needful matter through poverty of counsel. It was not the part of His kindly love that he who was to praise God's divine generosity in regard to others should be compelled to condemn it in regard to himself.

3. At last the best of artisans ordained that creature to whom He had been able to give nothing proper to himself should have joint possession of whatever had been peculiar to each of the different kinds of being. He therefore took man as a creature of indeterminate nature and, assigning him a place in the middle of the world, addressed him thus: "Neither a fixed abode nor a form that is thine alone nor any function peculiar to thyself have we given thee, Adam, to the end that according to thy longing and according to thy judgment thou mayest have and possess what abode, what form, and what functions thou thyself shalt desire. The nature of all other beings is limited and constrained within the bounds of laws prescribed by Us. Thou, constrained by no limits, in accordance with thine own free will, in whose hand We have placed thee, shalt ordain for thyself the limits of thy nature. We have set thee at the world's center that thou mayest from thence more easily observe whatever is in the world. We have made thee neither of heaven nor of earth, neither mortal nor immortal, so that with freedom of choice and with honor, as though the maker and molder of thyself, thou mayest fashion thyself in whatever shape thou shalt prefer. Thou shalt have the power to degenerate into the lower forms of life, which are brutish. Thou shalt have the power, out of thy soul's judgment, to be reborn into the higher forms, which are divine."

4. O supreme generosity of God the Father, O highest and most marvelous felicity of man! To him it is granted to have whatever he chooses, to be whatever he wills. Beasts as soon as they are born (so says Lucilius) bring with them from their mother's womb all they will ever possess. Spiritual beings, either from the beginning or soon thereafter, become what they are to be for ever and ever. On man when he came into life the Father conferred the seeds of all kinds and the germs of every way of life. Whatever seeds each man cultivates will grow to maturity and bear in him their own fruit. If they be vegetative, he will be like a plant. If sensitive, he will become brutish. If rational, he will grow into a heavenly being. If intellectual, he will be an angel and the son of God. And if, happy in the lot of no created thing, he withdraws into the center of his own unity, his spirit, made one with God, in the solitary darkness of God, who is set above all things, shall surpass them all. Who would not admire this our chameleon? Or who would more greatly admire aught else whatever? . . .

For it is not the bark that makes the plant but its senseless and insentient nature; neither is it the hide that makes the beast of burden but its irrational, sensitive soul; neither is it the orbed form that makes the heavens but their undeviating order; nor is it the sundering from body but his spiritual intelligence that makes the angel. For if you see one abandoned to his appetites crawling on the ground, it is a plant and not a man you see; if you see one blinded by the vain illusions of imagery, as it were of Calypso, and, softened by their gnawing allurement, delivered over to his senses, it is a beast and not a man you see. If you see a philosopher determining all things by means of right reason, him you shall reverence: he is a heavenly being and not of this earth. If you see a pure contemplator, one unaware of the body and confined to the inner reaches of the mind, he is neither an earthly nor a heavenly being: he is a more reverend divinity with human flesh.

Glossary

abode: dwelling place

admittedly: a short way of saying, "I admit that this may be."

adorned: decorated

allurement: attraction

archetype: the primary pattern or form according to which something is made.

artisan: craftsman

auditors: listeners

brutish: like brute beasts

chameleon: an animal that changes colors according to make it blend into its background.

confer: give, grant, bestow

constrained: held back, limited

contemplate: to look at in a reflective way

contemplator: one who contemplates

degenerate: to become lower, or one who is lower

determining: defining, giving clear outlines to

discernment: capacity to understand, to make out meaning

excrementary: having to do with excrement (shit)

felicity: happiness

indeterminate: without clear outlines, limits

insentient: unable to sense

intermediary: someone who mediates, or something which is in between

interval: a space between things

maturity: full development or the end point of growth

maxim: a saying, a moral saying

orbed: round-shaped like a ball

ordain: to command or decree, to devote to

peculiar to: special to, particular to

prescribed: required, demanded

quickened: given life

sensitive (as in sensitive soul): able to sense, having senses (like eyes, ears, nose, etc.)

sundering: separating, cutting apart

undeviating: not changing course, not veering off in other directions

vegetative: at the level of plant life

Hermes Trismegistus: The Renaissance was fascinated with books from the ancient world. Authorship was attributed to the Egyptian god of wisdom Thoth, the thrice great (tris—megistus). The Greek god Hermes was associated with the Egyptian god Thoth, hence Hermes Trismegistus. These ancient books dealt with magic, alchemy, astrology. These subjects were all the rage in the Renaissance. But the ancient works also dealt with the idea of a community, a unity, of all objects. Pico uses the phrase "the universal chain of Being."

Asclepius: the greek god of medicine.

Lucilius: Latin poet, often considered the founder of Latin Satire. He lived 150 years before Christ.

Calypso: a supernatural character in Homer's Odyssey who tried to make the Greek hero Odysseus stay with her on an island. She was a great temptress, skillful at creating illusions.

William Wordsworth (1770–1850), patriarch of English Romanticism, gives us no authorities to consider save our own senses. Look at Nature and learn! The first selection "Ode: Intimations of Immortality" appeared in 1807 in Poems in Two Volumes; *the second, "Tintern Abbey" appeared in 1798 in* Lyrical Ballads.

ODE

INTIMATIONS OF IMMORTALITY FROM RECOLLECTIONS OF EARLY CHILDHOOD

William Wordsworth

> *"The Child is father of the Man;*
> *And I could wish my days to be*
> *Bound each to each in natural piety."*

I

There was a time when meadow, grove, and stream,
The earth, and every common sight,
    To me did seem
    Apparelled in celestial light,
5   The glory and the freshness of a dream.
It is not now as it hath been of yore;—
    Turn wheresoe'er I may,
    By night or day,
The things which I have seen I now can see no more.

II

10   The Rainbow comes and goes,
    And lovely is the Rose,
    The Moon doth with delight
Look round her when the heavens are bare;
    Waters on a starry night
15   Are beautiful and fair;
    The sunshine is a glorious birth;
    But yet I know, where'er I go,
That there has past away a glory from the earth.

III

Now, while the birds thus sing a joyous song,
20   And while the young lambs bound
        As to the tabor's sound,
To me alone there came a thought of grief:
A timely utterance gave that thought relief,
        And I again am strong:
25 The cataracts blow their trumpets from the steep;
No more shall grief of mine the season wrong;
I hear the Echoes through the mountains throng,
The Winds come to me from the fields of sleep,
        And all the earth is gay;
30   Land and sea
    Give themselves up to jollity,
        And with the heart of May
Doth every beast keep holiday:—
        Thou Child of Joy,
35 Shout round me, let me hear thy shouts, thou happy
                            Shepherd-boy!

IV

Ye blessed Creatures, I have heard the call
    Ye to each other make; I see
The heavens laugh with you in your jubilee;
    My heart is at your festival,
40   My head hath its coronal,
The fullness of your bliss, I feel—I feel it all.
        Oh evil day! if I were sullen
        While Earth herself is adorning,
            This sweet May-morning,
45   And the children are culling
            On every side,
        In a thousand valleys far and wide,
        Fresh flowers; while the sun shines warm,
And the Babe leaps up on his mother's arm:—
50   I hear, I hear, with joy I hear!
        —But there's a Tree, of many, one,
A single Field which I have looked upon,

Both of them speak of something that is gone:
    The Pansy at my feet
55   Doth the same tale repeat:
Whither is fled the visionary gleam?
Where is it now, the glory and the dream?

V

Our birth is but a sleep and a forgetting:
The Soul that rises with us, our life's Star,
60   Hath had elsewhere its setting,
    And cometh from afar:
    Not in entire forgetfulness,
    And not in utter nakedness,
But trailing clouds of glory do we come
65   From God, who is our home:
Heaven lies about us in our infancy!
Shades of the prison-house begin to close
    Upon the growing Boy,
    But he
70 Beholds the light, and whence it flows,
    He sees in it his joy;
The Youth, who daily farther from the east
    Must travel, still is Nature's priest,
    And by the vision splendid
75   Is on his way attended;
At length the Man perceives it die away,
And fade into the light of common day.

VI

Earth fills her lap with pleasures of her own;
Yearnings she hath in her own natural kind,
80 And, even with something of a mother's mind,
    And no unworthy aim,
    The homely nurse doth all she can
To make her Foster-child, her inmate Man,
    Forget the glories he hath known,
85 And that imperial palace whence he came.

VII

Behold the Child among his new-born blisses,
A six years' darling of a pigmy size!
See, where 'mid work of his own hand he lies,
Fretted by sallies of his mother's kisses,
90   With light upon him from his father's eyes!
See, at his feet, some little plan or chart,
Some fragment from his dream of human life,
Shaped by himself with newly-learned art;
    A wedding or a festival,
95   A mourning or a funeral;
      And this hath now his heart,
      And unto this he frames his song:
        Then will he fit his tongue
To dialogues of business, love, or strife;
100   But it will not be long
    Ere this be thrown aside,
    And with new joy and pride
The little Actor cons another part;
Filling from time to time his 'humorous stage'
105   With all the Persons, down to palsied Age,
The life brings with her in her equipage;
    As if his whole vocation
    Were endless imitation.

VIII

Thou, whose exterior semblance doth belie
110   Thy soul's immensity;
Thou best philosopher, who yet dost keep
Thy heritage, thou eye among the blind,
That, deaf and silent, read'st the Eternal Deep,
Haunted forever by the Eternal Mind,—
115   Mighty prophet! seer blest!
    On whom those truths do rest,
Which we are toiling all our lives to find,
In darkness lost, the darkness of the grave;
Thou, over whom thy Immortality
120   Broods like the Day, a master o'er a slave,

A Presence which is not to be put by;
Thou little Child, yet glorious in the might
Of heaven-born freedom on thy being's height,
Why with such earnest pains doest thou provoke
125 The years to bring the inevitable yoke,
Thus blindly with thy blessedness at strife?
Full soon thy Soul shall have her earthly freight,
And custom lie upon thee with a weight,
Heavy as frost, and deep as life!

IX

130 O joy! that in our embers
Is something that doth live,
That nature yet remembers
What was so fugitive!
The thought of our past years in me doth breed
135 Perpetual benediction; not indeed
For that which is most worthy to be blest;
Delight and liberty, the simple creed
Of childhood, whether busy or at rest,
With new-fledged hope still fluttering in his breast:—
140 Nor for these I raise
The song of thanks and praise;
But for those obstinate questionings
Of sense and outward things,
Fallings from us, vanishings;
145 Blank misgivings of a Creature
Moving about in worlds not realized,
High instincts before which our mortal nature
Did tremble like a guilty thing surprised:
But for those first affections,
150 Those shadowy recollections,
Which, be they what they may,
Are yet the fountain-light of all our day,
Are yet a master-light of all our seeing;
Uphold us, cherish, and have power to make
155 Our noisy years seem moments in the being
Of the Eternal Silence: truths that wake,

To perish never:
Which neither listlessness, nor mad endeavor,
      Nor man nor boy,
160   Nor all that is at enmity with joy,
Can utterly abolish or destroy!
            Hence in a season of calm weather
            Though inland far we be,
Our souls have sight of that immortal sea
165   Which brought us hither,
            Can in a moment travel thither,
And see the children sport upon the shore,
And hear the mighty waters rolling evermore.

X

Then sing, ye Birds, sing, sing a joyous song!
170   And let the young Lambs bound
                  As to the tabor's sound!
We in thought will join your throng,
            Ye that pipe and ye that play,
            Ye that through your hearts to-day
175   Feel the gladness of the May!
What though the radiance which was once so bright
Be now forever taken from my sight,
            Though nothing can bring back the hour
Of splendor in the grass, or glory in the flower;
180   We will grieve not, rather find
                  Strength in what remains behind;
                  In the primal sympathy
                  Which having been must ever be;
                  In the soothing thoughts that spring
185   Out of human suffering;
                  In the faith that looks through death,
In years that bring the philosophic mind.

XI

And O, ye Fountains, Meadows, Hills, and Groves,
Forebode not any severing of our loves!
190   Yet in my heart of hearts I feel your might;
I only have relinquished one delight

To live beneath your more habitual sway.
I love the Brooks which down their channels fret,
Even more than when I tripped lightly as they;
195   The innocent brightness of a new-born Day
        Is lovely yet;
The Clouds that gather round the setting sun
Do take a sober colouring from an eye
That hath kept watch o'er man's mortality;
200   Another race hath been, and other palms are won.
Thanks to the human heart by which we live,
Thanks to its tenderness, its joys, and fears,
To me the meanest flower that blows can give
Thoughts that do often lie too deep for tears.

c. 1802–6

Lines Composed a Few Miles above Tintern Abbey, on Revisiting the Banks of the Wye During a Tour

William Wordsworth

Five years have past; five summers, with the length
Of five long winters! and again I hear
These waters, rolling from their mountain-springs
With a soft inland murmur.—Once again
5   Do I behold these steep and lofty cliffs,
That on a wild secluded scene impress
Thoughts of more deep seclusion; and connect
The landscape with the quiet of the sky.
The day is come when I again repose
10   Here, under this dark sycamore, and view
These plots of cottage-ground, these orchard-tufts,
Which at this season, with their unripe fruits,
Are clad in one green hue, and lose themselves
'Mid groves and copses. Once again I see
15   These hedge-rows, hardly hedge-rows, little lines
Of sportive wood run wild: these pastoral farms,
Green to the very door; and wreaths of smoke
Sent up, in silence from among the trees!
With some uncertain notice, as might seem
20   Of vagrant dwellers in the houseless woods,
Or of some Hermit's cave, where by his fire
The Hermit sits alone.
                              These beauteous forms,
Through a long absence, have not been to me
25   As is a landscape to a blind man's eye:
But oft, in lonely rooms, and 'mid the din
Of towns and cities, I have owed to them

In hours of weariness, sensations sweet,
Felt in the blood, and felt along the heart;
30   And passing even into my purer mind,
With tranquil restoration:—feelings too
Of unremembered pleasure: such, perhaps,
As have no slight or trivial influence
On the best portion of a good man's life,
35   His little, nameless, unremembered acts
Of kindness and of love. Nor less, I trust,
To them I may have owed another gift,
Of aspect more sublime: that blessed mood,
In which the burden of the mystery,
40   In which the heavy and weary weight
Of all this unintelligible world,
Is lightened:—that serene and blessed mood,
In which the affections gently lead us on,—
Until, the breath of this corporeal frame
45   And even the motion of our human blood
Almost suspended, we are laid asleep
In body, and become a living soul:
While with an eye made quiet by the power
Of harmony, and the deep power of joy,
50   We see into the life of things.
                                        If this
Be but a vain belief, yet, oh! how oft
In darkness and amid the many shapes
Of joyless daylight; when the fretful stir
55   Unprofitable, and the fever of the world,
Have hung upon the beatings of my heart—
How oft, in spirit, have I turned to thee,
O sylvan Wye! thou wanderer thro' the woods,
How often has my spirit turned to thee!
60   And now, with gleams of half extinguished thought,
With many recognitions dim and faint,
And somewhat of a sad perplexity,
The picture of the mind revives again:
While here I stand, not only with the sense
65   Of present pleasure, but with pleasing thoughts

That in this moment there is life and food
For Future years. And so I dare to hope,
Though changed, no doubt, from what I was when first
I came among these hills; when like a roe
70   I bounded o'er the mountains, by the sides
Of the deep rivers, and the lonely streams,
Wherever nature led: more like a man
Flying from something that he dreads, than one
Who sought the thing he loved. For nature then
75   (The coarser pleasures of my boyish days,
And their glad animal movements all gone by)
To me was all in all.—I cannot paint
What then I was. The sounding cataract
Haunted me like a passion: the tall rock,
80   The mountain, and the deep and gloomy wood,
Their colours and their forms, were then to me
An appetite; a feeling and a love,
That had no need of a remoter charm,
By thought supplied, nor any interest
85   Unborrowed from the eye.—That time is past,
And all its aching joys are now no more,
And all its dizzy raptures. Not for this
Faint I, nor mourn nor murmur; other gifts
Have followed; for such loss, I would believe,
90   Abundant recompense. For I have learned
To look on nature, not as in the hour
Of thoughtless youth; but hearing oftentimes
The still, sad music of humanity,
Nor harsh, nor grating, though of ample power
95   To chasten or subdue. And I have felt
A presence that disturbs me with the joy
Of elevated thoughts; a sense sublime
Of something far more deeply interfused,
Whose dwelling is the light of setting suns,
100   And the round ocean and the living air,
And the blue sky, and in the mind of man;
A motion and a spirit that impels
All thinking things, all objects of all thought,

And rolls through all things. Therefore am I still
105   A lover of the meadows and the woods,
And mountains; and of all that we behold
From this green earth; of all the mighty world
Of eye, and ear, —both what they half create,
And what perceive; well pleased to recognise
110   In nature and the language of the sense,
The anchor of my purest thoughts, the nurse,
The guide, the guardian of my heart, and soul
Of all my moral being.
                                        Nor perchance,
115   If I were not thus taught, should I the more
Suffer my genial spirits to decay:
For thou art with me here upon the banks
Of this fair river; thou my dearest Friend,
My dear, dear Friend; and in thy voice I catch
120   The language of my former heart, and read
My former pleasures in the shooting lights
Of thy wild eyes. Oh! yet a little while
May I behold in thee what I was once,
My dear, dear Sister! and this prayer I make,
125   Knowing that Nature never did betray
The heart that loved her; 'tis her privilege,
Through all the years of this our life, to lead
From joy to joy: for she can so inform
The mind that is within us, so impress
130   With quietness and beauty, and so feed
With lofty thoughts, that neither evil tongues,
Rash judgments, nor the sneers of selfish men,
Nor greetings where no kindness is, nor all
The dreary intercourse of daily life,
135   Shall e'er prevail against us, or disturb
Our cheerful faith that all which we behold
Is full of blessings. Therefore let the moon
Shine on thee in thy solitary walk;
And let the misty mountain-winds be free
140   To blow against thee: and, in after years,
When these wild ecstasies shall be matured

Into a sober pleasure; when thy mind
Shall be a mansion for all lovely forms,
Thy memory be as a dwelling-place
145 For all sweet sounds and harmonies; oh! then
If solitude, or fear, or pain, or grief,
Should be thy portion, with what healing thoughts
Of tender joy wilt thou remember me,
And these my exhortations! Nor, perchance—
150 If I should be where I no more can hear
Thy voice, nor catch from thy wild eyes these gleams
Of past existence—wilt thou then forget
That on the banks of this delightful stream
We stood together; and that I, so long
155 A worshipper of Nature, hither came
Unwearied in that service: rather say
With warmer love—oh! with far deeper zeal
Of holier love. Nor wilt thou then forget,
That after my wanderings, many years
160 Of absence, these steep woods and lofty cliffs,
And this green pastoral landscape, were to me
More dear, both for themselves and for thy sake!

July 13, 1798

*Buddhism, derived from the teachings of Siddhartha Gautama (563–483 B.C.E.),
is a rich and varied tradition. The following two selections from Japan represent
the Zen version of the tradition.*

*Buddhist understanding begins with the recognition that life is unfulfilling,
frustrating, and full of suffering. The reason is that our minds are clouded and
confused by unrealistic thoughts and futile desires. We are unwilling to accept the
reality of a world of constant change, where nothing lasts, and we cling to the
groundless belief that each of us has a core identity, a permanent self.*

*According to Buddhism, to clear the mind is to serenely see reality as it is, not
as we wish it to be. To free the mind is to understand there is no permanancy and
no permanent self, no self at all. The mind, emptied of all self-ness, of all self-
ishness, is the true mind. It is mindfulness—aware, attentive, clear.*

Rendell Mabey

Introducing Dōgen

The Zen master Dōgen (1200–1253), whom the Japanese Sōtō school regards
as its founder, was not only a deeply religious spiritual figure but also a profound and insightful thinker and an accomplished poet of nature. His most
explicitly philosophical work, the monumental *Shōbōgenzō* ("Treasury of the
True Dharma Eye"), is the first major Buddhist text to be written in Japanese
rather than classical Chinese as well as the first comprehensive work of philosophy in Japanese. It is an extremely dense and difficult text, over which
philosophers in Japan (and, more recently, in the West) have pondered long
and hard. As such, it does not lend itself to being excerpted and easily explained, so the passages from Dōgen that follow have been drawn from a more
accessible work, *Shōbōgenzō-Zuimonki*, a collection of stories and sayings from
Dōgen's life compiled by his disciple Ejō. (An excellent account of Dōgen's life
and thought can be found in Dumoulin's *Zen Buddhism: Japan*.)

The word "Zen" is ultimately derived from a Sanskrit term connoting
meditation, and while techniques of contemplation had been practiced for
some time in Japan, Dōgen revitalized the practice with his emphasis on *zazen*
("seated meditation"). Seated in a firm but relaxed cross-legged posture, with
the eyes open, one breathes through the nose and opens oneself to a prereflective,
nonconceptual awareness that Dōgen characterizes as "without-thinking." (See
Chapter 6 of Kasulis's *Zen Action/Zen Person* for an explanation of Dōgen's
notion of "without-thinking.") It is important that one sit simply as an ex-

pression of one's true nature, rather than *in order to* gain enlightenment. Proper practice will, however, result in what Dōgen calls "the molting of body-mind."

This last term, which could also be translated "body-heart," is intended to emphasize the unity of the physical and the psychical, to remind us that these are simply two aspects of our person rather than two separate components of the human being. As one of the passages excerpted below shows, Dōgen tends to view Zen practice as having even more to do with the body than the mind, and to see following "the Buddha Way" as a physical rather than simply mental activity. The Japanese term for "way" here is the same as the Chinese *tao* and is often used in Zen writings to stress that Zen practice is a matter of finding how to live one's own, unique life in harmony with the rest of the cosmos.

It will be helpful to mention two other ideas emphasized by Dōgen: impermanence and Buddha-nature. It is a central tenet of Buddhism that the world is basically impermanent, in the sense that all elements of existence are continually "arising and passing away." Buddhism suggests that the inherent "unsatisfactoriness" of existence is a result of the deep-rooted desire to grasp and hang on to the ephemerality of life. It sees the idea that there are enduring, self-identical things—including human egos or selves—as a pervasive illusion fabricated in an attempt to deny the radically ephemeral nature of existence. The full acknowledgment and experiential apreciation of impermanence takes one quite some distance along the Buddha Way.

The idea of Buddha-nature is more difficult, having to do with the fundamentally "enlightened" nature of everything in the world. Dōgen associates Buddha-nature with the central notion of later, Mahayana Buddhism, which is *sunyatā*: "nothingness" or "emptiness." The realization of the essential emptiness of all things has to do with seeing that nothing is what it is "in itself," that everything is what it is only in relation to other things. Thus Dōgen writes, "Buddha-nature is vast emptiness, open, clear, and bright." He extends the idea of Buddha-nature beyond all sentient beings to everything in the universe and claims that it is thus not different from impermanence. (This idea is the theme of a recent book by a Western philosopher, Joan Stambaugh: *Impermanence Is Buddha-Nature*.) Everything is, just as it is, perfectly enlightened; but this basic condition is obscured from us by layers of conceptualization and by discriminating consciousness which divides things into good and bad, beautiful and ugly, pleasurable and painful.

In one of the passages that follow, Dōgen admonishes his students: "Remember that you are alive only today in this moment." In other writings Dōgen develops some highly sophisticated ideas about time, which make it clear that there is more to enlightenment than simply "living in the moment"— which is something, after all, that animals manage effortlessly and without any trouble. Thanks to the complex temporal structure of human existence, when one manages to enter fully into the flow of impermanence, one finds that the past and future are somehow gathered up into every moment of the present. (Dōgen's ideas about time bear remarkable similarities to the thinking of some modern Western philosophers—namely, Kierkegaard, Nietzsche, and Heidegger—about the "moment.")

Dōgen Kigen Writes

Next, to arouse such an aspiration, think deeply in your heart of the impermanence of the world. It is not a matter of meditating using some provisional method of contemplation. It is not a matter of fabricating in our heads that which does not really exist. Impermanence is truly the reality right in front of our eyes. We need not wait for some teaching from others, proof from some passage of scripture, or some principle. Born in the morning, dead in the evening, a person we saw yesterday is no longer here today—these are the facts we see with our eyes and hear with our ears. This is what we see and hear about others. Applying this to our own bodies, and thinking of the reality (of all things), though we expect to live for seventy or eighty years, we die when we must die.

During our lifetime, though we may see the reality of sorrow, pleasure, love of our families, and hatred of our enemies, these are not worthy matters. We could spend our time letting go of them. We should just believe in the Buddha-Way and seek the true joy of Nirvana. Much more so for the aged whose lives are already more than half over. How many years still remain? How can we let up studying the Way? This is still not close enough to reality. In reality, it is only today or even this moment that we can thus think of worldly affairs or of the Buddha-Way. Tonight or tomorrow we may contract some serious disease, or may have to endure such terrible pain as to be unable to distinguish east from west. Or, we may be killed suddenly by some demon, encounter trouble with brigands, or be killed by some enemy. Everything is truly uncertain.

Therefore, in such an unpredictable world, it is extremely foolish to waste time worrying about various ways of earning a living in order to postpone one's death—uncertain as it is—to say nothing of plotting evil against others.

Precisely because this is reality, the Buddha preached it to all living beings, the patriarchs taught only this truth in their sermons and writings. In my formal speeches or lectures too, I emphasize that impermanence is swift; life-and-death is the great matter. Reflect on this reality again and again in your heart without forgetting it, and without wasting a moment. Put your whole mind into the practice of the Way. Remember that you are alive only today in this moment. Other than that, [practice of the Way] is truly easy. You needn't discuss whether you are superior or inferior, brilliant or dull.

Dōgen also said,

Is the Way attained through mind or body? in the teaching-schools, it is said that since body and mind are not separate, the Way is attained through the body. Yet, it is not clear that we attain the Way through the body, because they say "since" body and mind are not separate. In Zen, the Way is attained through both body and mind.

As long as we only think about the buddha-dharma with our minds, the Way will never be grasped, even in a thousand lifetimes or a myriad of eons. When we let go of our minds and cast aside our views and understandings, the Way will be actualized. One sage clarified True Mind (Reality) when he saw peach blossoms, and another realized the Way when he heard the sound of tile hitting a bamboo. They attained the Way through their bodies. Therefore, when we completely cast aside our thoughts and views and practice *shikantaza*, we will become intimate with the Way. For this reason, the Way is doubtlessly attained through the body. This is why I encourage you to practice zazen wholeheartedly.

Dōgen instructed,

Students of the Way, the reason you do not attain enlightenment is because you hold onto your old views. Without knowing who taught you, you think that "mind" is the function of your brain—thought and discrimination. When I tell you that "mind" is grass and trees, you do not believe it. When you talk about the Buddha you think the Buddha must have various physical characteristics and a radiant halo. If I say that the Buddha is broken tiles and pebbles, you show astonishment. The views you cling to are neither what has been transmitted to you from your father nor what you were taught by your mother. You have believed them for no particular reason; they are the result of having listened for a long time to what people have said. Therefore, since it is the definite word of the buddhas, and patriarchs, when it is said that "mind" is grass and trees, you should understand that grass and trees are "mind," and if you are told that "Buddha" is tiles and pebbles, you should believe that tiles and pebbles are the "Buddha." Thus, if you reform your attachment, you will be able to attain the Way.

Introducing Takuan Sōhō

The Zen master Takuan Sōhō (1573–1645) is the major representative at the beginning of the Edo period of the second main school of Japanese Zen, the Rinzai school. As well as being a Zen monk, Takuan was a talented scholar, poet, calligrapher, and adept of the tea ceremony. Since the medieval period in Japan, a number of schools of archery and swordsmanship, while informed primarily by Confucian virtues, had also been inspired by the spirit of Zen, so their members became well-versed in Zen practice. Through his friendship with the famous sword master Yagyū Munemori, Takuan was prompted to express a number of Zen teachings in the context of the art of swordsmanship. (A comprehensive account of the relation of Zen to swordsmanship can be found in D. T. Suzuki, *Zen and Japanese Culture*; see also the more nuanced treatment of Takuan by Dumoulin in in *Zen Buddhism: Japan*.)

While the Rinzai school of Zen accords with Dōgen in understanding the mind and body as an inseparable unity, Takuan's ideas about the Zen sword are in many respects exemplifications of Dōgen's idea that "the attainment of the Way is truly accomplished with the body." Takuan remarks an important analogy between Zen practice and the kind of physical discipline necessary for becoming a master of the sword. When the student first begins to learn, he tends to respond instinctively and without thinking (even if not very effectively) to an attack by an opponent. After a good amount of training in how to hold the sword and wield it, where to place the mind, and so on, he tends to be somewhat hampered by all the information and technique gained through the practice. But finally, after many more years of work, when the body's responses have been honed to the finest of edges, the student is able once again to respond and take action without thinking—but by now the technique has become flawless to the point of being almost super-human. As Takuan says: "When the highest perfection is attained, hands, feet, and all bodily members move by themselves, without any intervention from the mind."

In speaking about the heart-mind, Takuan uses two terms from the Chinese Zen tradition: "no mind" and "original mind" (translated as "right mind" in the excerpt that follows). The condition of "no mind" is attained through the elimination of all attachment to the world through conceptualization or representation, feelings and desires, prejudices and preconceptions. With the body's reflexes disciplined to perfection, and the mind thus emptied, one is able to respond appropriately to the new life situation of every moment with utter spontaneity. In an actual sword fight, the greatest obstacle to success may be the desire to beat the opponent or preserve one's life. Since the instinct for self-preservation is one of the deepest in all animals, the aim of the Zen art of the sword is shot through with paradox: by overcoming the desire to preserve himself, the sword master is free to act in totally open spontaneity—such that his life in fact is preserved after all. This is one of the major ideas behind the famous motto of Bushido, the way of the warrior: "The way of the samurai is the way of death." (Excerpts from the classic text of Bushido can be found in *Hagakure: The Book of the Samurai*; some reflections on the contemporary relevance of the book are contained in *Yukio Mishima on Hagakure: The Samurai Ethic and Modern Japan*.)

Takuan employs an image drawn from Taoism to describe the workings— or, better, the play—of what he calls "original mind": it must be like water (and not frozen like ice) so that it may flow immediately to whatever part of the body or the environment is apropriate at the moment. This is the image behind his emphasis in the excerpt that follows: one must never let the mind *stop* at anything, or disaster will ensue. The passage that follows is an extract from a letter to Yagyū Munemori, containing Zen reflections on the art in which his friend was so accomplished.

Takuan Sōhō Writes

Where One Puts the Mind

We say that:

If one puts his mind in the action of his opponent's body, his mind will be taken by the action of his opponent's body.

If he puts his mind in his opponent's sword, his mind will be taken by that sword.

If he puts his mind in thoughts of his opponent's intention to strike him, his mind will be taken by thoughts of his opponent's intention to strike him.

If he puts his mind in his own sword, his mind will be taken by his own sword.

If he puts his mind in his own intention of not being struck, his mind will be taken by his intention of not being struck.

If he puts his mind in the other man's stance, his mind will be taken by the other man's stance.

What this means is that there is no place to put the mind.

A certain person once said, "No matter where I put my mind, my intentions are held in check in the place where my mind goes, and I lose to my opponent. Because of that, I place my mind just below my navel and do not let it wander. Thus am I able to change according to the actions of my opponent."

This is reasonable. But viewed from the highest standpoint of Buddhism, putting the mind just below the navel and not allowing it to wander is a low level of understanding, not a high one. It is at the level of discipline and training. It is at the level of seriousness.

When a person does not think, "Where shall I put it?" the mind will extend throughout the entire body and move about to any place at all.

Not putting the mind anywhere, can't one use the mind, having it go from place to place, responding to the opponent's movements?

If the mind moves about the entire body, when the hand is called into action, one should use the mind that is in the hand. When the foot is called for, one should use the mind that is in the foot. But if you determine one place in which to put it, when you try to draw it out of that place, there it will stay. It will be without function.

Keeping the mind like a tied-up cat and not allowing it to wander, when you keep it in check within yourself, within yourself will it be detained. Forsaking it within your body, it will go nowhere.

The effort not to stop the mind in just one place—this is discipline. Not stoping the mind is object and essence. Put nowhere, it will be everywhere. Even in moving the mind outside the body, if it is sent in one direction, it will be lacking in nine others. If the mind is not restricted to just one direction, it will be in all ten.

In not remaining in one place, the Right Mind is like water. The Confused Mind is like ice, and ice is unable to wash hands or head. When ice is melted, it becomes water and flows everywhere, and it can wash the hands, the feet or anything else.

If the mind congeals in one place and remains with one thing, it is like frozen water and is unable to be used freely: ice that can wash neither hands nor feet. When the mind is melted and is used like water, extending throughout the body, it can be sent wherever one wants to send it.

This is the Right Mind.

The No-Mind is the same as the Right Mind. It neither congeals nor fixes itself in one place. It is called No-Mind when the mind has neither discrimination nor thought but wanders about the entire body and extends throughout the entire self.

The No-Mind is placed nowhere. Yet it is not like wood or stone. Where there is no stopping place, it is called No-Mind. When it stops, there is something in the mind. When there is nothing in the mind, it is called the mind of No-Mind. It is also called No-Mind-No-Thought.

When this No-Mind has been well developed, the mind does not stop with one thing nor does it lack any one thing. It is like water overflowing and exists within itself. It apears appropriately when facing a time of need.

The mind that becomes fixed and stops in one place does not function freely. Similarly, the wheels of a cart go around because they are not rigidly in place. If they were to stick tight, they would not go around. The mind is also something that does not function if it becomes attached to a single situation.

If there is some thought within the mind, though you listen to the words spoken by another, you will not really be able to hear him. This is because your mind has stopped with your own thoughts.

If your mind leans in the directions of these thoughts, though you listen, you will not hear; and though you look, you will not see. This is because there is something in your mind. What is there is thought. if you are able to remove this thing that is there, your mind will become No-Mind, it will function when needed, and it will be apropriate to its use.

The mind that thinks about removing what is within it will by the very act be occupied. If one will not think about it, the mind will remove these thoughts by itself and of itself become No-Mind.

I Stand Here Ironing

Tillie Olsen

I stand here ironing, and what you asked me moves tormented back and forth with the iron.

"I wish you would manage the time to come in and talk with me about your daughter. I'm sure you can help me understand her. She's a youngster who needs help and whom I'm deeply interested in helping."

"Who needs help." . . . Even if I came, what good would it do? You think because I am her mother I have a key, or that in some way you could use me as a key? She has lived for nineteen years. There is all that life that has happened outside of me, beyond me.

And when is there time to remember, to sift, to weigh, to estimate, to total? I will start and there will be an interruption and I will have to gather it all together again. Or I will become engulfed with all I did or did not do, with what should have been and what cannot be helped.

She was a beautiful baby. The first and only one of our five that was beautiful at birth. You do not guess how new and uneasy her tenancy in her now-loveliness. You did not know her all those years she was thought homely, or see her poring over her baby pictures, making me tell her over and over how beautiful she had been—and would be, I would tell her—and was now, to the seeing eye. But the seeing eyes were few or nonexistent. Including mine.

I nursed her. They feel that's important nowadays. I nursed all the children, but with her, with all the fierce rigidity of first motherhood, I did like the books then said. Though her cries battered me to trembling and my breasts ached with swollenness, I waited till the clock decreed.

Why do I put that first? I do not even know if it matters, or if it explains anything.

She was a beautiful baby. She blew shining bubbles of sound. She loved motion, loved light, loved color and music and textures. She would lie on the floor in her blue overalls patting the surface so hard in ecstasy her hands and feet would blur. She was a miracle to me, but when she was eight months old

I had to leave her daytimes with the woman downstairs to whom she was no miracle at all, for I worked or looked for work and for Emily's father, who "could no longer endure" (he wrote in his good-bye note) "sharing want with us."

I was nineteen. It was the pre-relief, pre-WPA world of the depression. I would start running as soon as I got off the streetcar, running up the stairs, the place smelling sour, and awake or asleep to startle awake, when she saw me she would break into a clogged weeping that could not be comforted, a weeping I can hear yet.

After a while I found a job hashing at night so I could be with her days, and it was better. But it came to where I had to bring her to his family and leave her.

It took a long time to raise the money for her fare back. Then she got chicken pox and I had to wait longer. When she finally came, I hardly knew her, walking quick and nervous like her father, looking like her father, thin, and dressed in a shoddy red that yellowed her skin and glared at the pock-marks. All the baby loveliness gone.

She was two. Old enough for nursery school they said, and I did not know then what I know now—the fatigue of the long day, and the lacerations of group life in the kinds of nurseries that are only parking places for children.

Except that it would have made no difference if I had known. It was the only place there was. It was the only way we could be together, the only way I could hold a job.

And even without knowing, I knew. I knew the teacher that was evil be-cause all these years it has curdled into my memory, the little boy hunched in the corner, her rasp, "why aren't you outside, because Alvin hits you? that's no reason, go out, scaredy." I knew Emily hated it even if she did not clutch and implore "don't go Mommy" like the other children, mornings.

She always had a reason why we should stay home. Momma, you look sick. Momma, I feel sick. Momma, the teachers aren't there today, they're sick. Momma, we can't go, there was a fire there last night. Momma, it's a holiday today, no school, they told me.

But never a direct protest, never rebellion. I think of our others in their three-, four-year-oldness—the explosions, the tempers, the denunciations, the demands—and I feel suddenly ill. I put the iron down. What in me demanded that goodness in her? And what was the cost, the cost to her of such goodness?

The old man living in the back once said in his gentle way: "You should smile at Emily more when you look at her." What *was* in my face when I looked at her? I loved her. There were all the acts of love.

It was only with the others I remembered what he said, and it was the face of joy, and not of care or tightness or worry I turned to them—too late for Emily. She does not smile easily, let alone almost always as her brothers and sisters do. Her face is closed and sombre, but when she wants, how fluid. You must have seen it in her pantomimes, you spoke of her rare gift for comedy on the stage that rouses a laughter out of the audience so dear they applaud and applaud and do not want to let her go.

Where does it come from, that comedy? There was none of it in her when she came back to me that second time, after I had had to send her away again. She had a new daddy now to learn to love, and I think perhaps it was a better time.

Except when we left her alone nights, telling ourselves she was old enough.

"Can't you go some other time, Mommy, like tomorrow?" she would ask. "Will it be just a little while you'll be gone? Do you promise?"

The time we came back, the front door open, the clock on the floor in the hall. She rigid awake. "It wasn't just a little while. I didn't cry. Three times I called you, just three times, and then I ran downstairs to open the door so you could come faster. The clock talked loud. I threw it away, it scared me what it talked."

She said the clock talked loud again that night I went to the hospital to have Susan. She was delirious with the fever that comes before red measles, but she was fully conscious all the week I was gone and the week after we were home when she could not come near the new baby or me.

She did not get well. She stayed skeleton thin, not wanting to eat, and night after night she had nightmares. She would call for me, and I would rouse from exhaustion to sleepily call back: "You're all right, darling, go to sleep, it's just a dream," and if she still called, in a sterner voice, "now go to sleep, Emily, there's nothing to hurt you." Twice, only twice, when I had to get up for Susan anyhow, I went in to sit with her.

Now when it is too late (as if she would let me hold and comfort her like I do the others) I get up and go to her at once at her moan or restless stirring.

"Are you awake, Emily? Can I get you something?" And the answer is always the same: "No, I'm all right, go back to sleep, Mother."

They persuaded me at the clinic to send her away to a convalescent home in the country where "she can have the kind of food and care you can't manage for her, and you'll be free to concentrate on the new baby." They still send children to that place. I see pictures on the society page of sleek young women planning affairs to raise money for it, or dancing at the affairs, or decorating Easter eggs or filling Christmas stockings for the children.

They never have a picture of the children so I do not know if the girls still wear those gigantic red bows and the ravaged looks on the every other Sunday when parents can come to visit "unless otherwise notified"—as we were notified the first six weeks.

Oh it is a handsome place, green lawns and tall trees and fluted flower beds. High up on the balconies of each cottage the children stand, the girls in their red bows and white dresses, the boys in white suits and giant red ties. The parents stand below shrieking up to be heard and the children shriek down to be heard, and between them the invisible wall "Not To Be Contaminated by Parental Germs or Physical Affection."

There was a tiny girl who always stood hand in hand with Emily. Her parents never came. One visit she was gone. "They moved her to Rose Cottage" Emily shouted in explanation. "They don't like you to love anybody here."

She wrote once a week, the labored writing of a seven-year-old. "I am fine. How is the baby. If I write my leter nicly I will have a star. Love." There never was a star. We wrote every other day, letters she could never hold or keep but only hear read—once. "We simply do not have room for children to keep any personal possessions," they patiently explained when we pieced one Sunday's shrieking together to plead how much it would mean to Emily, who loved so to keep things, to be allowed to keep her letters and cards.

Each visit she looked frailer. "She isn't eating," they told us.

(They had runny eggs for breakfast or mush with lumps, Emily said later, I'd hold it in my mouth and not swallow. Nothing ever tasted good, just when they had chicken.)

It took us eight months to get her released home, and only the fact that she gained back so little of her seven lost pounds convinced the social worker.

I used to try to hold and love her after she came back, but her body would stay stiff, and after a while she'd push away. She ate little. Food sickened her, and I think much of life too. Oh she had physical lightness and brightness, twinkling by on skates, bouncing like a ball up and down up and down over the jump rope, skimming over the hill; but these were momentary.

She fretted about her appearance, thin and dark and foreign-looking at a time when every little girl was supposed to look or thought she should look a chubby blonde replica of Shirley Temple. The doorbell sometimes rang for her, but no one seemed to come and play in the house or be a best friend. Maybe because we moved so much.

There was a boy she loved painfully through two school semesters. Months later she told me how she had taken pennies from my purse to buy him candy. "Licorice was his favorite and I brought him some every day, but he still liked Jennifer better'n me. Why, Mommy?" The kind of question for which there is no answer.

School was a worry to her. She was not glib or quick in a world where glibness and quickness were easily confused with ability to learn. To her overworked and exasperated teachers she was an overconscientious "slow learner" who kept trying to catch up and was absent entirely too often.

I let her be absent, though sometimes the illness was imaginary. How different from my now-strictness about attendance with the others. I wasn't working. We had a new baby, I was home anyhow. Sometimes, after Susan grew old enough, I would keep her home from school, too, to have them all together.

Mostly Emily had asthma, and her breathing, harsh and labored, would fill the house with a curiously tranquil sound. I would bring the two old dresser mirrors and her boxes of collections to her bed. She would select beads and single earrings, bottle tops and shells, dried flowers and pebbles, old postcards and scraps, all sorts of oddments; then she and Susan would play Kingdom, setting up landscapes and furniture, peopling them with action.

Those were the only times of peaceful companionship between her and Susan. I have edged away from it, that poisonous feeling between them, that terrible balancing of hurts and needs I had to do between the two, and did so badly, those earlier years.

Oh there are conflicts between the others too, each one human, needing, demanding, hurting, taking—but only between Emily and Susan, no, Emily toward Susan that corroding resentment. It seems so obvious on the surface, yet it is not obvious. Susan, the second child, Susan, golden- and curly-haired and chubby, quick and articulate and assured, everything in appearance and manner Emily was not; Susan, not able to resist Emily's precious things, losing or sometimes clumsily breaking them; Susan telling jokes and riddles to company for applause while Emily sat silent (to say to me later: that was *my* riddle, Mother, I told it to Susan); Susan, who for all the five years' difference in age was just a year behind Emily in developing physically.

I am glad for that slow physical development that widened the difference between her and her contemporaries, though she suffered over it. She was too vulnerable for that terrible world of youthful competition, of preening and parading, of constant measuring of yourself against every other, of envy, "If I had that copper hair," "If I had that skin. . . ." She tormented herself enough about not looking like the others, there was enough of the unsureness, the having to be conscious of words before you speak, the constant caring—what are they thinking of me? without having it all magnified by the merciless physical drives.

Ronnie is calling. He is wet and I change him. It is rare there is such a cry now. That time of motherhood is almost behind me when the ear is not one's own but must always be racked and listening for the child cry, the child call. We sit for a while and I hold him, looking out over the city spread in charcoal with its soft aisles of light. "*Shoogily,*" he breathes and curls closer. I carry him back to bed, asleep. *Shoogily.* A funny word, a family word, inherited from Emily, invented by her to say: *comfort.*

In this and other ways she leaves her seal, I say aloud. And startle at my saying it. What do I mean? What did I start to gather together, to try and make coherent? I was at the terrible, growing years. War years. I do not remember them well. I was working, there were four smaller ones now, there was not time for her. She had to help be a mother, and housekeeper, and shopper. She had to set her seal. Mornings of crisis and near hysteria trying to get lunches packed, hair combed, coats and shoes found, everyone to school or Child Care on time, the baby ready for transportation. And always the paper scribbled on by a smaller one, the book looked at by Susan then mislaid, the homework not done. Running out to that huge school where she was one, she was lost, she was a drop; suffering over her unpreparedness, stammering and unsure in her classes.

There was so little time left at night after the kids were bedded down. She would struggle over books, always eating (it was in those years she developed her enormous appetite that is legendary in our family) and I would be ironing, or preparing food for the next day, or writing V-mail to Bill, or tending the baby. Sometimes, to make me laugh, or out of her despair, she would imitate happenings or types at school.

I think I said once: "Why don't you do something like this in the school amateur show?" One morning she phoned me at work, hardly understandable through the weeping: "Mother, I did it. I won, I won; they gave me first prize; they clapped and clapped and wouldn't let me go."

Now suddenly she was Somebody, and as imprisoned in her difference as she had been in her anonymity.

She began to be asked to perform at other high schools, even in colleges, then at city and statewide affairs. The first one we went to, I only recognized her that first moment when thin, shy, she almost drowned herself into the curtains. Then: Was this Emily? The control, the command, the convulsing and deadly clowning, the spell, then the roaring, stamping audience, unwilling to let this rare and precious laughter out of their lives.

Afterwards: You ought to do something about her with a gift like that— but without money or knowing how, what does one do? We have left it all to her, and the gift has as often eddied inside, clogged and clotted, as been used and growing.

She is coming. She runs up the stairs two at a time with her light graceful step, and I know she is happy tonight. Whatever it was that occasioned your call did not happen today.

"Aren't you ever going to finish the ironing, Mother? Whistler painted his mother in a rocker. I'd have to paint mine standing over an ironing board." This is one of her communicative nights and she tells me everything and nothing as she fixes herself a plate of food out of the icebox.

She is so lovely. Why did you want me to come in at all? Why were you concerned? She will find her way.

She starts up the stairs to bed. "Don't get *me* up with the rest in the morning." "But I thought you were having midterms." "Oh, those," she comes back in, kisses me, and says quite lightly, "in a couple of years when we'll all be atom-dead they won't matter a bit."

She has said it before. She *believes* it. But because I have been dredging the past, and all that compounds a human being is so heavy and meaningful in me, I cannot endure it tonight.

I will never total it all. I will never come in to say: She was a child seldom smiled at. Her father left me before she was a year old. I had to work away from her her first six years when there was work, or I sent her home and to his relatives. There were years she had care she hated. She was dark and thin and foreign-looking in a world where the prestige went to blondeness and curly hair and dimples, she was slow where glibness was prized. She was a child of anxious, not proud, love. We were poor and could not afford for her the soil of easy growth. I was a young mother, I was a distracted mother. There were the other children pushing up, demanding. Her younger sister seemed all that she was not. There were years she did not let me touch her. She kept too much in herself, her life was such she had to keep too much in herself. My wisdom came too late. She has much to her and probably little will come of it. She is a child of her age, of depression, of war, of fear.

Let her be. So all that is in her will not bloom—but in how many does it? There is still enough left to live by. Only help her to know—help make it so there is cause for her to know—that she is more than this dress on the ironing board, helpless before the iron.

Tell Me a Riddle

Tillie Olsen

1

For forty-seven years they had been married. How deep back the stubborn, gnarled roots of the quarrel reached, no one could say—but only now, when tending to the needs of others no longer shackled them together, the roots swelled up visible, split the earth between them, and the tearing shook even to the children, long since grown.

Why now, why now? wailed Hannah.

As if when we grew up weren't enough, said Paul.

Poor Ma. Poor Dad. It hurts so for both of them, said Vivi. They never had very much; at least in old age they should be happy.

Knock their heads together, insisted Sammy; tell 'em: you're too old for this kind of thing; no reason not to get along now.

Lennie wrote to Clara: They've lived over so much together; what could possibly tear them apart?

Something tangible enough.

Arthritic hands, and such work as he got, occasional. Poverty all his life, and there was little breath left for running. He could not, could not turn away from this desire: to have the troubling of responsibility, the fretting with money, over and done with; to be free, to be *care*free where success was not measured by accumulation, and there was use for the vitality still in him.

There was a way. They could sell the house, and with the money join his lodge's Haven, cooperative for the aged. Happy communal life, and was he not already an official; had he not helped organize it, raise funds, served as a trustee?

But she—would not consider it.

83

"What do we need all this for?" he would ask loudly, for her hearing aid was turned down and the vacuum was shrilling. "Five rooms" (pushing the sofa so she could get into the corner) "furniture" (smoothing down the rug) "floors and surfaces to make work. Tell me, why do we need it?" And he was glad he could ask in a scream.

"Because I'm use't."

"Because you're use't. This is a reason, Mrs. Word Miser? Used to can get unused!"

"Enough unused I have to get used to already. . . . Not enough words?" turning off the vacuum a moment to hear herself answer. "Because soon enough we'll need only a little closet, no windows, no furniture, nothing to make work, but for worms. Because now I want room. . . . Screech and blow like you're doing, you'll need that closet even sooner. . . . Ha, again!" for the vacuum bag wailed, puffed half up, hung stubbornly limp. "This time fix it so it stays; quick before the phone rings and you get too important-busy."

But while he struggled with the motor, it seethed in him, Why fix it? Why have to bother? And if it can't be fixed, have to wring the mind with how to pay the repair? At the Haven they come in with their own machines to clean your room or your cottage; you fish, or play cards, or make jokes in the sun, not with knotty fingers fight to mend vacuums.

Over the dishes, coaxingly: "For once in your life, to be free, to have everything done for you, like a queen."

"I never liked queens."

"No dishes, no garbage, no towel to sop, no worry what to buy, what to eat."

"And what else would I do with my empty hands? Better to eat at my own table when I want, and to cook and eat how I want."

"In the cottages they buy what you ask, and cook it how you like. *You* are the one who always used to say: better mankind born without mouths and stomachs than always to worry for money to buy, to shop, to fix, to cook, to wash, to clean."

"How cleverly you hid that you heard, I said it then because eighteen hours a day I ran. And you never scraped a carrot or knew a dish towel sops. Now—for you and me—who cares? A herring out of a jar is enough. But when *I* want, and nobody to bother." And she turned off her ear button, so she would not have to hear.

But as *he* had no peace, juggling and rejuggling the money to figure: how will I pay for this now?; prying out the storm windows (there they take care of this); jolting in the streetcar on errands (there I would not have to ride to take care of this or that); fending the patronizing relatives just back from Florida (at the Haven it matters what one is, not what one can afford), he gave *her* no peace.

"Look! In their bulletin. A reading circle. Twice a week it meets."

"Haumm," her answer of not listening.

"A reading circle. Chekhov they read that you like, and Peretz. Cultured people at the Haven that you would enjoy."

"Enjoy!" She tasted the word. "Now, when it pleases you, you find a reading circle for me. And forty years ago when the children were morsels and there was a Circle, did you stay home with them once so I could go? Even once? You trained me well. I do not need others to enjoy. Others!" Her voice trembled. "Because *you* want to be there with others. Already it makes me sick to think of you always around others. Clown, grimacer, floormat, yesman, entertainer, whatever they want of you."

And now it was he who turned on the television loud so he need not hear.

Old scar tissue ruptured and the wounds festered anew. Chekhov indeed. She thought without softness of that young wife, who in the deep night hours while she nursed the current baby, and perhaps held another in her lap, would try to stay awake for the only time there was to read. She would feel again the weather of the outside on his cheek when, coming late from a meeting, he would find her so, and stimulated and ardent, sniffing her skin, coax: "I'll put the baby to bed, and you—put the book away, don't read, don't read."

That had been the most beguiling of all the "don't read, put your book away" her life had been. Chekhov indeed!

"Money?" She shrugged him off. "Could we get poorer than once we were? And in America, who starves?"

But as still he pressed:

"Let me alone about money. Was there ever enough? Seven little ones— for every penny I had to ask—and sometimes, remember, there was nothing. But always *I* had to manage. Now *you* manage. Rub your nose in it good."

But from those years she had had to manage, old humiliations and terrors rose up, lived again, and forced her to relive them. The children's needings;

that grocer's face or this merchant's wife she had had to beg credit from when credit was a disgrace; the scenery of the long blocks walked around when she could not pay; school coming, and the desperate going over the old to see what could yet be remade; the soups of meat bones begged "for-the-dog" one winter. . . .

Enough. Now they had no children. Let *him* wrack his head for how they would live. She would not exchange her solitude for anything. *Never again to be forced to move to the rhythms of others.*

For in this solitude she had won to a reconciled peace.

Tranquillity from having the empty house no longer an enemy, for it stayed clean—not as in the days when it was her family, the life in it, that had seemed the enemy: tracking, smudging, littering, dirtying, engaging her in endless defeating battle—and on whom her endless defeat had been spewed.

The few old books, memorized from rereading; the pictures to ponder (the magnifying glass superimposed on her heavy eyeglasses). Or if she wishes, when he is gone, the phonograph, that if she turns up very loud and strains, she can hear: the ordered sounds and the struggling.

Out in the garden, growing things to nurture. Birds to be kept out of the pear tree, and when the pears are heavy and ripe, the old fury of work, for all must be canned, nothing wasted.

And her one social duty (for she will not go to luncheons or meetings) the boxes of old clothes left with her, as with a life-practised eye for finding what is still wearable within the worn (again the magnifying glass superimposed on the heavy glasses) she scans and sorts—this for rag or rummage, that for mending and cleaning, and this for sending away.

Being able at last to live within, and not move to the rhythms of others, as life had forced her to: denying; removing; isolating; taking the children one by one; then deafening, half-blinding—and at last, presenting her solitude.

And in it she had won to a reconciled peace.

Now he was violating it with his constant campaigning: *Sell the house and move to the Haven.* (You sit, you sit—there too you could sit like a stone.) He was making of her a battleground where old grievances tore. (Turn on your ear button—I am talking.) And stubbornly she resisted—so that from wheedling, reasoning, manipulation, it was bitterness he now started with.

And it came to where every happening lashed up a quarrel.

"I will sell the house anyway," he flung at her one night. "'I am putting it up for sale. There will be a way to make you sign."

The television blared, as always it did on the evenings he stayed home, and as always it reached her only as noise. She did not know if the tumult was in her or outside. Snap! she turned the sound off. "Shadows," she whispered to him, pointing to the screen, "look, it is only shadows." And in a scream: "Did you say that you will sell the house? Look at me, not at that. I am no shadow. You cannot sell without me."

"Leave on the television. I am watching."

"Like Paulie, like Jenny, a four-year-old. Staring at shadows. *You cannot sell the house.*" .

"I will. We are going to the Haven. There you would not hear the television when you do not want it. I could sit in the social room and watch. You could lock yourself up to smell your unpleasantness in a room by yourself— for who would want to come near you?"

"No, no selling." A whisper now.

"The television is shadows. Mrs. Enlightened! Mrs. Cultured! A world comes into your house—and it is shadows. People you would never meet in a thousand lifetimes. Wonders. When you were four years old, yes, like Paulie, like Jenny, did you know of Indian dances, alligators, how they use bamboo in Malaya? No, you scratched in your dirt with the chickens and thought Olshana was the world. Yes, Mrs. Unpleasant, I will sell the house, for there better can we be rid of each other than here."

She did not know if the tumult was outside, or in her. Always a ravening inside, a pull to the bed, to lie down, to succumb.

"Have you thought maybe Ma should let a doctor have a look at her?" asked their son Paul after Sunday dinner, regarding his mother crumpled on the couch, instead of, as was her custom, busying herself in Nancy's kitchen.

"Why not the President too?"

"Seriously, Dad. This is the third Sunday she's lain down like that after dinner. Is she that way at home?"

"A regular love affair with the bed. Every time I start to talk to her."

Good protective reaction, observed Nancy to herself. The workings of hos-til-ity.

"Nancy could take her. I just don't like how she looks. Let's have Nancy arrange an appointment."

"You think she'll go?" regarding his wife gloomily. "All right, we have to have doctor bills, we have to have doctor bills." Loudly: "Something hurts you?"

She startled, looked to his lips. He repeated: "Mrs. Take It Easy, something hurts?"

"Nothing. . . . Only you."

"A woman of honey. That's why you're lying down?"

"Soon I'll get up to do the dishes, Nancy."

"Leave them, Mother, I like it better this way."

"Mrs. Take It Easy, Paul says you should start ballet. You should go to see a doctor and ask: how soon can you start ballet?"

"A doctor?" she begged. "Ballet?"

"We were talking, Ma," explained Paul, "you don't seem any too well. It would be a good idea for you to see a doctor for a checkup."

"I get up now to do the kitchen. Doctors are bills and foolishness, my son. I need no doctors."

"At the Haven," he could not resist pointing out, "a doctor is *not* bills. He lives beside you. You start to sneeze, he is there before you open up a Kleenex. You can be sick there for free, all you want."

"Diarrhea of the mouth, is there a doctor to make you dumb?"

"Ma. Promise me you'll go. Nancy will arrange it."

"It's all of a piece when you think of it," said Nancy, "the way she attacks my kitchen, scrubbing under every cup hook, doing the inside of the oven so I can't enjoy Sunday dinner, knowing that half-blind or not, she's going to find every speck of dirt. . . ."

"Don't, Nancy, I've told you—it's the only way she knows to be useful. What did the *doctor* say?"

"A real fatherly lecture. Sixty-nine is young these days. Go out, enjoy life, find interests. Get a new hearing aid, this one is antiquated. Old age is sickness only if one makes it so. Geriatrics, Inc."

"So there was nothing physical."

"Of course there was. How can you live to yourself like she does without there being? Evidence of a kidney disorder, and her blood count is low. He gave her a diet, and she's to come back for follow-up and lab work. . . . But he was clear enough: Number One prescription—start living like a human being. . . . When I think of your dad, who could really play the invalid with that arthritis of his, as active as a teenager, and twice as much fun. . . ."

"You didn't tell me the doctor says your sickness is in you, how you live." He pushed his advantage. "Life and enjoyments you need better than medicine. And this diet, how can you keep it? To weigh each morsel and scrape away each bit of fat, to make this soup, that pudding. There, at the Haven, they have a dietician, they would do it for you."

She is silent.

"You would feel better there, I know it," he says gently. "There there is life and enjoyments all around."

"What is the matter, Mr. Importantbusy, you have no card game or meeting you can go to?"—turning her face to the pillow.

For a while he cut his meetings and going out, fussed over her diet, tried to wheedle her into leaving the house, brought in visitors:

"I should come to a fashion tea. I should sit and look at pretty babies in clothes I cannot buy. This is pleasure?"

"Always you are better than everyone else. The doctor said you should go out. Mrs. Brem comes to you with goodness and you turn her away."

"Because *you* asked her to, she asked me."

"They won't come back. People you need, the doctor said. Your own cousins I asked; they were willing to come and make peace as if nothing had happened. . . ."

"No more crushers of people, pushers, hypocrites, around me. No more in *my* house. You go to them if you like."

"Kind he is to visit. And you, like ice."

"A babbler. All my life around babblers. Enough!"

"She's even worse, Dad? Then let her stew a while," advised Nancy. "You can't let it destroy you; it's a psychological thing, maybe too far gone for any of us to help."

So he let her stew. More and more she lay silent in bed, and sometimes did not even get up to make the meals. No longer was the tongue-lashing inevitable if he left the coffee cup where it did not belong, or forgot to take out the garbage or mislaid the broom. The birds grew bold that summer and for once pocked the pears, undisturbed.

A bellyful of bitterness and every day the same quarrel in a new way and a different old grievance the quarrel forced her to enter and relive. And the new torment: I am not really sick, the doctor said it, then why do I feel so sick?

One night she asked him: "You have a meeting tonight? Do not go. Stay . . . with me."

He had planned to watch "This Is Your Life," but half sick himself from the heavy heat, and sickening therefore the more after the brooks and woods of the Haven, with satisfaction he grated:

"Hah, Mrs. Live Alone And Like It wants company all of a sudden. It doesn't seem so good the time of solitary when she was a girl exile in Siberia. 'Do not go. Stay with me.' A new song for Mrs. Free As A Bird. Yes, I am going out, and while I am gone chew this aloneness good, and think how you keep us both from where if you want people, you do not need to be alone."

"Go, go. All your life you have gone without me."

After him she sobbed curses he had not heard in years, old-country curses from their childhood: Grow, oh shall you grow like an onion, with your head in the ground. Like the hide of a drum shall you be, beaten in life, beaten in death. Oh shall you be like a chandelier, to hang, and to burn. . . .

She was not in their bed when he came back. She lay on the cot on the sun porch. All week she did not speak or come near him; nor did he try to make peace or care for her.

He slept badly, so used to her next to him. After all the years, old harmonies and dependencies deep in their bodies; she curled to him, or he coiled to her, each warmed, warming, turning as the other turned, the nights a long embrace.

It was not the empty bed or the storm that woke him, but a faint singing. *She* was singing. Shaking off the drops of rain, the lightning riving her lifted face, he saw her so; the cot covers on the floor.

"This is a private concert?" he asked. "Come in, you are wet."

"I can breathe now," she answered; "my lungs are rich." Though indeed the sound was hardly a breath.

"Come in, come in." Loosing the bamboo shades. "Look how wet you are." Half helping, half carrying her, still faint-breathing her song.

A Russian love song of fifty years ago.

He had found a buyer, but before he told her, he called together those children who were close enough to come. Paul, of course, Sammy from New Jersey, Hannah from Connecticut, Vivi from Ohio.

With a kindling of energy for her beloved visitors, she arrayed the house, cooked and baked. She was not prepared for the solemn after-dinner conclave, they too probing in and tearing. Her frightened eyes watched from mouth to mouth as each spoke.

His stories were eloquent and funny of her refusal to go back to the doctor; of the scorned invitations; of her stubborn silence or the bile "like a Niagara"; of her contrariness: "If I clean it's no good how I cleaned; if I don't clean, I'm still a master who thinks he has a slave."

(Vinegar he poured on me all his life; I am well marinated; how can I be honey now?)

Deftly he marched in the rightness for moving to the Haven; their money from social security free for visiting the children, not sucked into daily needs and into the house; the activities in the Haven for him; but mostly the Haven for *her:* her health, her need of care, distraction, amusement, friends who shared her interests.

"This does offer an outlet for Dad," said Paul; "he's always been an active person. And economic peace of mind isn't to be sneezed at, either. I could use a little of that myself."

But when they asked: "And you, Ma, how do you feel about it?" could only whisper:

"For him it is good. It is not for me. I can no longer live between people."

"You lived all your life *for* people," Vivi cried.

"Not with." Suffering doubly for the unhappiness on her children's faces.

"You have to find some compromise," Sammy insisted. "Maybe sell the house and buy a trailer. After forty-seven years there's surely some way you can find to live in peace."

"There is no help, my children. Different things we need."

"Then live alone!" He could control himself no longer. "I have a buyer for the house. Half the money for you, half for me. Either alone or with me to the Haven. You think I can live any longer as we are doing now?"

"Ma doesn't have to make a decision this minute, however you feel, Dad," Paul said quickly, "and you wouldn't want her to. Let's let it lay a few months, and then talk some more."

"I think I can work it out to take Mother home with me for a while," Hannah said. "You both look terrible, but especially you, Mother. I'm going to ask Phil to have a look at you."

"Sure," cracked Sammy. "What's the use of a doctor husband if you can't get free service out of him once in a while for the family? And absence might make the heart . . . you know."

"There was something after all," Paul told Nancy in a colorless voice. "That was Hannah's Phil calling. Her gall bladder. . . . Surgery."

"Her *gall* bladder. If that isn't classic. 'Bitter as gall'—talk of psychosom—"

He stepped closer, put his hand over her mouth, and said in the same colorless, plodding voice. "We have to get Dad. They operated at once. The cancer was everywhere, surrounding the liver, everywhere. They did what they could . . . at best she has a year. Dad . . . we have to tell him."

2

Honest in his weakness when they told him, and that she was not to know. "I'm not an actor. She'll know right away by how I am. Oh that poor woman. I am old too, it will break me into pieces. Oh that poor woman. She will spit on me: 'So my sickness was how I live.' Oh Paulie, how she will be, that poor woman. Only she should not suffer. . . . I can't stand sickness, Paulie, I can't go with you."

But went. And play-acted.

"A grand opening and you did not even wait for me. . . .A good thing Hannah took you with her."

"Fashion teas I needed. They cut out what tore in me; just in my throat something hurts yet. . . . Look! so many flowers, like a funeral. Vivi called, did Hannah tell you? And Lennie from San Francisco, and Clara; and Sammy is coming." Her gnome's face pressed happily into the flowers.

It is impossible to predict in these cases, but once over the immediate effects of the operation, she should have several months of comparative well-being.

> *The money, where will come the money?*

Travel with her, Dad. Don't take her home to the old associations. The other children will want to see her.

> *The money, where will I wring the money?*

Whatever happens, she is not to know. No, you can't ask her to sign papers to sell the house; nothing to upset her. Borrow instead, then after. . . .

> *I had wanted to leave you each a few dollars to make life easier, as other fathers do. There will be nothing left now. (Failure! you and your "business is exploitation." Why didn't you make it when it could be made?—Is that what you're thinking of me, Sammy?)*

Sure she's unreasonable, Dad—but you have to stay with her; if there's to be any happiness in what's left of her life, it depends on you.

> *Prop me up, children, think of me, too. Shuffled, chained with her, bitter woman. No Haven, and the little money going. . . . How happy she looks, poor creature.*

The look of excitement. The straining to hear everything (the new hearing aid turned full). Why are you so happy, dying woman?

How the petals are, fold on fold, and the gladioli color. The autumn air.

Stranger grandsons, tall above the little gnome grandmother, the little spry grandfather. Paul in a frenzy of picture-taking before going.

She, wandering the great house. Feeling the books; laughing at the maple shoemaker's bench of a hundred years ago used as a table. The ear turned to music.

"Let us go home. See how good I walk now." "One step from the hospital," he answers, "and she wants to fly. Wait till Doctor Phil says."

"Look—the birds too are flying home. Very good Phil is and will not show it, but he is sick of sickness by the time he comes home."

"Mrs. Telepathy, to read minds," he answers; "read mine what it says: when the trunks of medicines become a suitcase, then we will go."

The grandboys, they do not know what to say to us. . . . Hannah, she runs around here, there, when is there time for herself?

Let us go home. Let us go home.

Musing; gentleness—*but for the incidents of the rabbi in the hospital, and of the candles of benediction.*

Of the rabbi in the hospital:

Now tell me what happened, Mother.

From the sleep I awoke, Hannah's Phil, and he stands there like a devil in a dream and calls me by name. I cannot hear. I think he prays. Go away, please, I tell him, I am not a believer. Still he stands, while my heart knocks with fright.

You scared *him*, Mother. He thought you were delirious.

Who sent him? Why did he come to *me*?

It is a custom. The men of God come to visit those of their religion they might help. The hospital makes up the list for them—race, religion— and you are on the Jewish list.

Not for rabbis. At once go and make them change. Tell them to write: Race, human; Religion, none.

And of the candles of benediction:

Look how you have upset yourself, Mrs. Excited Over Nothing. Pleasant memories you should leave.

Go in, go back to Hannah and the lights. Two weeks I saw candles and said nothing. But she asked me.

So what was so terrible? She forgets you never did, she asks you to light the Friday candles and say the benediction like Phil's mother when she visits. If the candles give her pleasure, why shouldn't she have the pleasure?

Not for pleasure she does it. For emptiness. Because his family does. Because all around her do.

That is not a good reason too? But you did not hear her. For heritage, she told you. For the boys, from the past they should have tradition.

Superstition! From our ancestors, savages, afraid of the dark, of themselves: mumbo words and magic lights to scare away ghosts.

She told you: how it started does not take away the goodness. For centuries, peace in the house it means.

Swindler! does she look back on the dark centuries? Candles bought instead of bread and stuck into a potato for a candlestick? Religion that stifled and said: in Paradise, woman, you will be the footstool of your husband, and in life—poor chosen Jew—ground under, despised, trembling in cellars. And cremated. And cremated.

This is religion's fault? You think you are still an orator of the 1905 revolution? Where are the pills for quieting? Which are they?

Heritage. How have we come from our savage past, how no longer to be savages—this to teach. To look back and learn what humanizes—this to teach. To smash all ghettos that divide us—not to go back, not to go back—this to teach. Learned books in the house, will humankind live or die, and she gives to her boys—superstition.

Hannah that is so good to you. Take your pill, Mrs. Excited For Nothing, swallow.

Heritage! But when did I have time to teach? Of Hannah I asked only hands to help.

Swallow.

Otherwise—musing; gentleness.

Not to travel. To go home.

The children want to see you. We have to show them you are as thorny a flower as ever.

Not to travel.

Vivi wants you should see her new baby. She sent the tickets—airplane tickets—a Mrs. Roosevelt she wants to make of you. To Vivi's we have to go.

A new baby. How many warm, seductive babies. She holds him stiffly, *away* from her, so that he wails. And a long shudder begins, and the sweat beads on her forehead.

"Hush, shush," croons the grandfather, lifting him back. "You should forgive your grandmamma, little prince, she has never held a baby before, only seen them in glass cases. Hush, shush."

"You're tired, Ma," says Vivi. "The travel and the noisy dinner. I'll take you to lie down."

(A long travel from, to, what the feel of a baby evokes.)

In the airplane, cunningly designed to encase from motion (no wind, no feel of flight), she had sat severely and still, her face turned to the sky through which they cleaved and left no scar.

So this was how it looked, the determining, the crucial sky, and this was how man moved through it, remote above the dwindled earth, the concealed human life. Vulnerable life, that could scar.

There was a steerage ship of memory that shook across a great, circular sea: clustered, ill human beings; and through the thick-stained air, tiny fretting waters in a window round like the airplane's—sun round, moon round.

(The round thatched roofs of Olshana.) Eye round—like the smaller window that framed distance the solitary year of exile when only her eyes could travel, and no voice spoke. And the polar winds hurled themselves across snows trackless and endless and white—like the clouds which had closed together below and hidden the earth.

Now they put a baby in her lap. Do not ask me, she would have liked to beg. Enough the worn face of Vivi, the remembered grandchildren. I cannot, cannot. . . .

Cannot what? Unnatural grandmother, not able to make herself embrace a baby.

She lay there in the bed of the two little girls, her new hearing aid turned full, listening to the sound of the children going to sleep, the baby's fretful crying and hushing, the clatter of dishes being washed and put away. They thought she slept. Still she rode on.

It was not that she had not loved her babies, her children. The love—the passion of tending—had risen with the need like a torrent; and like a torrent drowned and immolated all else. But when the need was done—oh the power that was lost in the painful damming back and drying up of what still surged, but had nowhere to go. Only the thin pulsing left that could not quiet, suffering over lives one felt, but could no longer hold nor help.

On that torrent she had borne them to their own lives, and the riverbed was desert long years now. Not there would she dwell, a memoried wraith. Surely that was not all, surely there was more. Still the springs, the springs were in her seeking. Somewhere an older power that beat for life. Somewhere coherence, transport, meaning. If they would but leave her in the air now stilled of clamor, in the reconciled solitude, to journey on.

And they put a baby in her lap. Immediacy to embrace, and the breath of *that* past: warm flesh like this that had claims and nuzzled away all else and with lovely mouths devoured; hot-living like an animal—intensely and now; the turning maze; the long drunkenness; the drowning into needing and being needed. Severely she looked back—and the shudder seized her again, and the sweat. Not that way. Not there, not now could she, not yet. . . .

And all that visit, she could not touch the baby.

"Daddy, is it the . . . sickness she's like that?" asked Vivi. "I was so glad to be having the baby—for her. I told Tim, it'll give her more happiness than anything, being around a baby again. And she hasn't played with him once."

He was not listening, "Aahh little seed of life, little charmer," he crooned, "Hollywood should see you. A heart of ice you would melt. Kick, kick. The future you'll have for a ball. In 2050 still kick. Kick for your grandaddy then."

Attentive with the older children; sat through their performances (command performance; we command you to be the audience); helped Ann sort autumn leaves to find the best for a school program; listened gravely to Richard tell about his rock collection, while her lips mutely formed the words to remember: *igneous, sedimentary, metamorphic;* looked for missing socks, books, and bus tickets; watched the children whoop after their grandfather who knew how to tickle, chuck, lift, toss, do tricks, tell secrets, make jokes, match riddle for riddle. (Tell me a riddle, Grammy. I know no riddles, child.) Scrubbed sills and woodwork and furniture in every room; folded the laundry; straightened drawers; emptied the heaped baskets waiting for ironing (while he or Vivi or Tim nagged: You're supposed to rest here, you've been sick) but to none tended or gave food—and could not touch the baby.

After a week she said: "Let us go home. Today call about the tickets."

"You have important business, Mrs. Inahurry? The President waits to consult with you?" He shouted, for the fear of the future raced in him. "The clothes are still warm from the suitcase, your children cannot show enough how glad they are to see you, and you want home. There is plenty of time for home. We cannot be with the children at home."

"Blind to around you as always: the little ones sleep four in a room because we take their bed. We are two more people in a house with a new baby, and no help."

"Vivi is happy so. The children should have their grandparents a while, she told to me. I should have my mommy and daddy. . . ."

"Babbler and blind. Do you look at her so tired? How she starts to talk and she cries? I am not strong enough yet to help. Let us go home."

(To reconciled solitude.)

For it seemed to her the crowded noisy house was listening to her, listening for her. She could feel it like a great ear pressed under her heart. And everything knocked: quick constant raps: let me in, let me in.

How was it that soft reaching tendrils also became blows that knocked?

C'mon, Grandma, I want to show you. . . .

Tell me a riddle, Grandma. (*I know no riddles.*)

Look, Grammy, he's so dumb he can't even find his hands. (Dody and the baby on a blanket over the fermenting autumn mould.)

I made them—for you. (Ann) (Flat paper dolls with aprons that lifted on scalloped skirts that lifted on flowered pants; hair of yarn and great ringed questioning eyes.)

Watch me, Grandma. (Richard snaking up the tree, hanging exultant, free, with one hand at the top. Below Dody hunching over in pretend-cooking.) (*Climb too, Dody, climb and look.*)

Be my nap bed, Grammy. (The "No!" too late.) Morty's abandoned heaviness, while his fingers ladder up and down her hearing-aid cord to his drowsy chant: eentsiebeentsiespider. (*Children trust.*)

It's to start off your own rock collection, Grandma. That's a trilobite fossil, 200 million years old (millions of years on a boy's mouth) and that one's obsidian, black glass.

Knocked and knocked.

Mother, I *told* you the teacher said we had to bring it back all filled out this morning. Didn't you even ask Daddy? Then tell *me* which plan and I'll check it: evacuate or stay in the city or wait for you to come and take me away. (Seeing the look of straining to hear.) It's for Disaster, Grandma. (*Children trust.*)

Vivi in the maze of the long, the lovely drunkenness. The old old noises: baby sounds; screaming of a mother flayed to exasperation; children quarreling; children playing; singing; laughter.

And Vivi's tears and memories, spilling so fast, half the words not understood.

She had started remembering out loud deliberately, so her mother would know the past was cherished, still lived in her.

Nursing the baby: My friends marvel, and I tell them, oh it's easy to be such a cow. I remember how beautiful my mother seemed nursing my brother, and the milk just flows. . . . Was that Davy? It must have been Davy. . . .

Lowering a hem: How did you ever . . . when I think how you made everything we wore . . . Tim, just think, seven kids and Mommy sewed everything . . . do I remember you sang while you sewed? That white dress with the red apples on the skirt you fixed over for me, was it Hannah's or Clara's before it was mine?

Washing sweaters: Ma, I'll never forget, one of those days so nice you washed clothes outside; one of the first spring days it must have been. The bubbles just danced while you scrubbed, and we chased after, and you stopped to show us how to blow our own bubbles with green onion stalks . . . you always. . . .

"Strong onion, to still make you cry after so many years," her father said, to turn the tears into laughter.

While Richard bent over his homework: Where is it now, do we still have it, the Book of the Martyrs? It always seemed so, well—exalted, when you'd put it on the round table and we'd all look at it together; there was even a halo from the lamp. The lamp with the beaded fringe you could move up and down; they're in style again, pulley lamps like that, but without the fringe. You know the book I'm talking about, Daddy, the Book of the Martyrs, the first picture was a bust of Spartacus . . . Socrates? I wish there was something like that for the children, Mommy, to give them what you. . . . (And the tears splashed again.)

(What I intended and did not? Stop it, daughter, stop it, leave that time. And he, the hyprocrite, sitting there with tears in his eyes—it was nothing to you then, nothing.)

. . . The time you came to school and I almost died of shame because of your accent and because I knew you knew I was ashamed; how could I? . . . Sammy's harmonica and you danced to it once, yes you did, you and Davy squealing in your arms. . . . That time you bundled us up and walked us down to the railway station to stay the night 'cause it was heated and we didn't have any coal, that winter of the strike, you didn't think I remembered that, did you, Mommy? . . . How you'd call us out to see the sunsets. . . .

Day after day, the spilling memories. Worse now, questions, too. Even the grandchildren: Grandma, in the olden days, when you were little. . . .

It was the afternoons that saved.

While they thought she napped, she would leave the mosaic on the wall (of children's drawings, maps, calendars, pictures, Ann's cardboard dolls with their great ringed questioning eyes) and hunch in the girls' closet on the low shelf where the shoes stood, and the girls' dresses covered.

For that while she would painfully sheathe against the listening house, the tendrils and noises that knocked, and Vivi's spilling memories. Sometimes it helped to braid and unbraid the sashes that dangled, or to trace the pattern on the hoop slips.

Today she had jacks and children under jet trails to forget. Last night, Ann and Dody silhouetted in the window against a sunset of flaming man-made clouds of jet trail, their jacks ball accenting the peaceful noise of dinner being made. Had she told them, yes she had told them of how they played jacks in her village though there was no ball, no jacks. Six stones, round and flat, toss them out, the seventh on the back of the hand, toss, catch and swoop up as many as possible, toss again. . . .

Of stones (repeating Richard) there are three kinds: earth's fire jetting; rock of layered centuries; crucibled new out of the old (*igneous, sedimentary, metamorphic*). But there was that other—frozen to black glass, never to transform or hold the fossil memory . . . (let not my seed fall on stone). There was an ancient man who fought to heights a great rock that crashed back down eternally—eternal labor, freedom, labor . . . (stone will perish, but the word remain). And you, David, who with a stone slew, screaming: Lord, take my heart of stone and give me flesh

Who was screaming? Why was she back in the common room of the prison, the sun motes dancing in the shafts of light, and the informer being brought in, a prisoner now, like themselves. And Lisa leaping, yes, Lisa, the gentle and tender, biting at the betrayer's jugular. Screaming and screaming.

No, it is the children screaming. Another of Paul and Sammy's terrible fights?

In Vivi's house. Severely: you are in Vivi's house.

Blows, screams, a call: "Grandma!" For her? Oh please not for her. Hide, hunch behind the dresses deeper. But a trembling little body hurls itself beside her—surprised, smothered laughter, arms surround her neck, tears rub dry on her cheek, and words too soft to understand whisper into her ear (Is this where you hide too, Grammy? It's my secret place, we have a secret now).

And the sweat beads, and the long shudder seizes.

It seemed the great ear pressed inside now, and the knocking. "We have to go home," she told him, "I grow ill here."

"It's your own fault, Mrs. Bodybusy, you do not rest, you do too much." He raged, but the fear was in his eyes. "It was a serious operation, they told you to take care. . . . All right, we will go to where you can rest."

But where? Not home to death, not yet. He had thought to Lennie's, to Clara's; beautiful visits with each of the children. She would have to rest first, be stronger. If they could but go to Florida—it glittered before him, the never-realized promise of Florida. California: of course. (The money, the money, dwindling!) Los Angeles first for sun and rest, then to Lennie's in San Francisco.

He told her the next day. "You saw what Nancy wrote: snow and wind back home, a terrible winter. And look at you—all bones and a swollen belly. I called Phil: he said: 'A prescription, Los Angeles sun and rest.'"

She watched the words on his lips. "You have sold the house," she cried, "that is why we do not go home. That is why you talk no more of the Haven, why there is money for travel. After the children you will drag me to the Haven."

"The Haven! Who thinks of the Haven any more?

Tell her, Vivi, tell Mrs. Suspicious: a prescription, sun and rest, to make you healthy. . . . And how could I sell the house without *you?*"

At the place of farewells and greetings, of winds of coming and winds of going, they say their good-byes.

They look back at her with the eyes of others before them: Richard with her own blue blaze; Ann with the nordic eyes of Tim; Morty's dreaming brown of a great-grandmother he will never know; Dody with the laughing eyes of him who had been her springtide love (who stands beside her now); Vivi's, all tears.

The baby's eyes are closed in sleep.

Good-bye, my children.

3

It is to the back of the great city he brought her, to the dwelling places of the cast-off old. Bounded by two lines of amusement piers to the north and to the south, and between a long straight paving rimmed with black benches facing the sand—sands so wide the ocean is only a far fluting.

In the brief vacation season, some of the boarded stores fronting the sands open, and families, young people and children, may be seen. A little tasselled tram shuttles between the piers, and the lights of roller coasters prink and tweak over those who come to have sensation made in them.

The rest of the year it is abandoned to the old, all else boarded up and still; seemingly empty, except the occasional days and hours when the sun, like a tide, sucks them out of the low rooming houses, casts them onto the benches and sandy rim of the walk—and sweeps them into decaying enclosures once again.

A few newer apartments glint among the low bleached squares. It is in one of these Lennie's Jeannie has arranged their rooms. "Only a few miles north and south people pay hundreds of dollars a month for just this gorgeous air, Grandaddy, just this ocean closeness."

She had been ill on the plane, lay ill for days in the unfamiliar room. Several times the doctor came by—left medicine she would not take. Several times Jeannie drove in the twenty miles from work, still in her Visiting Nurse uniform, the lightness and brightness of her like a healing.

"Who can believe it is winter?" he asked one morning. "Beautiful it is outside like an ad. Come, Mrs. Invalid, come to taste it. You are well enough to sit in here, you are well enough to sit outside. The doctor said it too."

But the benches were encrusted with people, and the sands at the sidewalk's edge. Besides, she had seen the far ruffle of the sea: "there take me," and though she leaned against him, it was she who led.

Plodding and plodding, sitting often to rest, he grumbling. Patting the sand so warm. Once she scooped up a handful, cradling it close to her better eye; peered, and flung it back. And as they came almost to the brink and she could see the glistening wet, she sat down, pulled off her shoes and stockings, left him and began to run. "You'll catch cold," he screamed, but the sand in his shoes weighed him down—he who had always been the agile one—and already the white spray creamed her feet.

He pulled her back, took a handkerchief to wipe off the wet and the sand. "Oh no," she said, "the sun will dry," seized the square and smoothed it flat, dropped on it a mound of sand, knotted the kerchief corners and tied it to a bag—"to look at with the strong glass" (for the first time in years explaining an action of hers)—and lay down with the little bag against her cheek, looking toward the shore that nurtured life as it first crawled toward consciousness the millions of years ago.

He took her one Sunday in the evil-smelling bus, past flat miles of blister houses, to the home of relatives. Oh what is this? she cried as the light began to smoke and the houses to dim and recede. Smog, he said, everyone knows but you. . . . Outside he kept his arms about her, but she walked with hands pushing the heavy air as if to open it, whispered: who has done this? sat down suddenly to vomit at the curb and for a long while refused to rise.

One's age as seen on the altered face of those known in youth. Is this they he has come to visit? This Max and Rose, smooth and pleasant, introducing them to polite children, disinterested grandchildren, "the whole family, once a month on Sundays. And why not? We have the room, the help, the food."

Talk of cars, of houses, of success: this son that, that daughter this. And *your* children? Hastily skimped over, the intermarriages, the obscure work—" "my doctor son-in-law, Phil"—all he has to offer. She silent in a corner. (Carsick like a baby, he explains.) Years since he has taken her to visit anyone but the children, and old apprehensions prickle: "no incidents," he silently begs, "no incidents." He itched to tell them. "A very sick woman," significantly, indicating her with his eyes, "a very sick woman." Their restricted faces did not react. "Have you thought maybe she'd do better at Palm Springs?" Rose asked. "Or at least a nicer section of the beach, nicer people, a pool." Not to have to say "money" he said instead: "would she have sand to look at through a magnifying glass?" and went on, detail after detail, the old habit betraying of parading the queerness of her for laughter.

After dinner—the others into the living room in men- or women-clusters, or into the den to watch TV—the four of them alone. She sat close to him, and did not speak. Jokes, stories, people they had known, beginning of reminiscence, Russia fifty-sixty years ago. Strange words across the Duncan Phyfe table: *hunger; secret meetings; human rights; spies; betrayals; prison; escape*—interrupted by one of the grandchildren: "Commercial's on; any Coke left? Gee, you're missing a real hair-raiser." And then a granddaughter (Max proudly: "look at her, an American queen") drove them home on her way back to U.C.L.A. No incident—except that there had been no incidents.

The first few mornings she had taken with her the magnifying glass, but he would sit only on the benches, so she rested at the foot, where slatted bench shadows fell, and unless she turned her hearing aid down, other voices invaded.

Now on the days when the sun shone and she felt well enough, he took her on the tram to where the benches ranged in oblongs, some with tables for checkers or cards. Again the blanket on the sand in the striped shadows, but she no longer brought the magnifying glass. He played cards, and she lay in the sun and looked towards the waters; or they walked—two blocks down to the scaling hotel, two blocks back—past chili-hamburger stands, open-doored bars, Next -to- New and perpetual rummage sale stores.

Once, out of the aimless walkers, slow and shuffling like themselves, someone ran unevenly towards them, embraced, kissed, wept: "dear friends, old friends." A friend of *hers*, not his: Mrs. Mays who had lived next door to them in Denver when the children were small.

Thirty years are compressed into a dozen sentences; and the present, not even in three. All is told: the children scattered; the husband dead; she lives in a room two blocks up from the sing hall—and points to the domed auditorium jutting before the pier. The leg? phlebitis; the heavy breathing? that, one does not ask. She, too, comes to the benches each day to sit. And tomorrow, tomorrow, are they going to the community sing? Of course he would have heard of it, everybody goes—the big doings they wait for all week. They have never been? She will come to them for dinner tomorrow and they will all go together.

So it is that she sits in the wind of the singing, among the thousand various faces of age.

She had turned off her hearing aid at once they came into the auditorium—as she would have wished to turn off sight.

One by one they streamed by and imprinted on her—and though the savage zest of their singing came voicelessly soft and distant, the faces still roared—the faces densened the air—chorded into

children-chants, mother-croons, singing of the chained
love serenades, Beethoven storms, mad Lucia's scream
drunken joy-songs, keens for the dead, work-singing

while from floor to balcony to dome a bare-footed sore-covered little girl threaded the soundthronged tumult, danced her ecstasy of grimace to flutes that scratched at a cross-roads village wedding

Yes, faces became sound, and the sound became faces; and faces and sound became weight—pushed, pressed

"Air"—her hands claw his.

"Whenever I enjoy myself. . . ." Then he saw the gray sweat on her face. "Here. Up. Help me, Mrs. Mays," and they support her out to where she can gulp the air in sob after sob.

"A doctor, we should get for her a doctor."

"Tch, it's nothing," says Ellen Mays, "I get it all the time. You've missed the tram; come to my place. Fix your hearing aid, honey . . . close . . . tea. My view. See, she *wants* to come. Steady now, that's how." Adding mysteriously: "Remember your advice, easy to keep your head above water, empty things float. Float."

The singing a fading march for them, tall woman with a swollen leg, weaving little man, and the swollen thinness they help between.

The stench in the hall: mildew? decay? "We sit and rest then climb. My gorgeous view. We help each other and here we are."

The stench along into the slab of room. A washstand for a sink, a box with oilcloth tacked around for a cupboard, a three-burner gas plate. Artificial flowers, colorless with dust. Everywhere pictures foaming: wedding, baby, party, vacation, graduation, family pictures. From the narrow couch under a slit of window, sure enough the view: lurching rooftops and a scallop of ocean heaving, preening, twitching under the moon.

"While the water heats. Excuse me . . . down the hall." Ellen Mays has gone.

"You'll live?" he asks mechanically, sat down to feel his fright; tried to pull her alongside.

She pushed him away. "For air," she said; stood clinging to the dresser. Then, in a terrible voice:

After a lifetime of room. Of many rooms.

Shhh.

You remember how she lived. Eight children. And now one room   like a coffin.

She pays rent!

Shrinking the life of her   into one room   like a coffin   Rooms and rooms like this   I lie on the quilt and hear them talk

Please, Mrs. Orator-without-Breath.

Once you went for coffee   I walked   I saw   A Balzac   a Chekhov to write it   Rummage   Alone   On scraps

Better old here than in the old country!

On scraps   Yet they sang like   Wondrous!

Humankind   *one has to believe*   So strong   For what? To rot   not grow?

Your poor lungs beg you. They sob between each word.

Singing.   Unused   the life in them.   She   in this poor room   with her pictures   Max   You   The   children   Everywhere unused the life And who has meaning?   Century after century   still all in us   not   to grow?

Coffins, rummage, plants: sick woman. Oh lay down. We will get for you the doctor.

"And when will it end. Oh, *the end*." *That* nightmare thought, and this time she writhed, crumpled against him, seized his hand (for a moment again the weight, the soft distant roaring of humanity) and on the strangled-for breath, begged: "Man . . . we'll destroy ourselves?"

And looking for answer—in the helpless pity and fear for her (for *her*) that distorted his face—she understood the last months, and knew that she was dying.

4

"Let us go home," she said after several days.

"You are in training for a cross-country run? That is why you do not even walk across the room? Here, like a prescription Phil said, till you are stronger from the operation. You want to break doctor's orders?"

She saw the fiction was necessary to him, was silent; then: "At home I will get better. If the doctor here says?"

"And winter? And the visits to Lennie and to Clara? All right," for he saw the tears in her eyes, "I will write Phil, and talk to the doctor."

Days passed. He reported nothing. Jeannie came and took her out for air, past the boarded concessions, the hooded and tented amusement rides, to the end of the pier. They watched the spent waves feeding the new, the gulls in the clouded sky; even up where they sat, the wind-blown sand stung.

She did not ask to go down the crooked steps to the sea.

Back in her bed, while he was gone to the store, she said: "Jeannie, this doctor, he is not one I can ask questions. Ask him for me, can I go home?"

Jeannie looked at her, said quickly: "Of course, poor Granny. You want your own things around you, don't you? I'll call him tonight. . . . Look, I've something to show you," and from her purse unwrapped a large cookie, intricately shaped like a little girl. "Look at the curls—can you hear me well, Granny?—and the darling eyelashes. I just came from a house where they were baking them."

"The dimples, there in the knees," she marveled, holding it to the better light, turning, studying, "like art. Each singly they cut, or a mold?"

"Singly," said Jeannie, "and if it is a child only the mother can make them. Oh Granny, it's the likeness of a real little girl who died yesterday—Rosita. She was three years old. *Pan del Muerto*, the Bread of the Dead. It was the custom in the part of Mexico they came from."

Still she turned and inspected. "Look, the hollow in the throat, the little cross necklace. . . . I think for the mother it is a good thing to be busy with such bread. You know the family?"

Jeannie nodded. "On my rounds. I nursed. . . . Oh Granny, it is like a party; they play songs she liked to dance to. The coffin is lined with pink velvet and she wears a white dress. There are candles. . . ."

"In the house?" Surprised, "They keep her in the house?"

"Yes," said Jeannie, "and it *is* against the health law. The father said it will be sad to bury her in this country; in Oaxaca they have a feast night with candles each year; everyone picnics on the graves of those they loved until dawn."

"Yes, Jeannie, the living must comfort themselves." And closed her eyes.

"You want to sleep, Granny?"

"Yes, tired from the pleasure of you. I may keep the Rosita? There stand it, on the dresser, where I can see; something of my own around me."

In the kitchenette, helping her grandfather unpack the groceries, Jeannie said in her light voice:

"I'm resigning my job, Grandaddy."

"Ah, the lucky young man. Which one is he?"

"Too late. You're spoken for." She made a pyramid of cans, unstacked, and built again.

"Something is wrong with the job?"

"With me. I can't be"—she searched for the word—"What they call professional enough. I let myself feel things. And tomorrow I have to report a family. . . ." The cans clicked again. "It's not that, either. I just don't know what I want to do, maybe go back to school, maybe go to art school. I thought if you went to San Francisco I'd come along and talk it over with Momma and Daddy. But I don't see how you can go. She wants to go home. She asked me to ask the doctor."

The doctor told her himself. "Next week you may travel, when you are a little stronger." But next week there was the fever of an infection, and by the time that was over, she could not leave the bed—a rented hospital bed that stood beside the double bed he slept in alone now.

Outwardly the days repeated themselves. Every other afternoon and evening he went out to his newfound cronies, to talk and play cards. Twice a week, Mrs. Mays came. And the rest of the time, Jeannie was there.

By the sickbed stood Jeannie's FM radio. Often into the room the shapes of music came. She would lie curled on her side, her knees drawn up, intense in listening (Jeannie sketched her so, coiled, convoluted like an ear), then thresh her hand out and abruptly snap the radio mute—still to lie in her attitude of listening, concealing tears.

Once Jeannie brought in a young Marine to visit, a friend from high-school days she had found wandering near the empty pier. Because Jeannie asked him to, gravely, without self-consciousness, he sat himself crosslegged on the floor and performed for them a dance of his native Samoa.

Long after they left, a tiny thrumming sound could be heard where, in her bed, she strove to repeat the beckon, flight, surrender of his hands, the fluttering footbeats, and his low plaintive calls.

Hannah and Phil sent flowers. To deepen her pleasure, he placed one in her hair. "Like a girl," he said, and brought the hand mirror so she could see. She looked at the pulsing red flower, the yellow skull face; a desolate, excited laugh shuddered from her, and she pushed the mirror away—but let the flower burn.

The week Lennie and Helen came, the fever returned. With it the excited laugh, and incessant words. She, who in her life had spoken but seldom and then only when necessary (never having learned the easy, social uses of words), now in dying, spoke incessantly.

In a half-whisper: "Like Lisa she is, your Jeannie. Have I told you of Lisa who taught me to read? Of the highborn she was, but noble in herself. I was sixteen; they beat me; my father beat me so I would not go to her. It was forbidden, she was a Tolstoyan. At night, past dogs that howled, terrible dogs, my son, in the snows of winter to the road, I to ride in her carriage like a lady, to books. To her, life was holy, knowledge was holy, and she taught me to read. They hung her. Everything that happens one must try to understand why. She killed one who betrayed many. Because of betrayal, betrayed all she lived and believed. In one minute she killed, before my eyes (there is so much blood in a human being, my son), in prison with me. All that happens, one must try to understand.

"The name?" Her lips would work. "The name that was their pole star; the doors of the death houses fixed to open on it; I read of it my year of penal servitude. Thuban!" very excited, "Thuban, in ancient Egypt the pole star. Can you see, look out to see it, Jeannie, if it swings around *our* pole star that seems to *us* not to move.

"Yes, Jeannie, at your age my mother and grandmother had already buried children . . . yes, Jeannie, it is more than oceans between Olshana and you . . . yes, Jeannie, they danced, and for all the bodies they had they might as well be chickens, and indeed, they scratched and flapped their arms and hopped.

"And Andrei Yefimitch, who for twenty years had never known of it and never wanted to know, said as if he wanted to cry: but why my dear friend this malicious laughter?" Telling to herself half-memorized phrases from her few books. "Pain I answer with tears and cries, baseness with indignation, meanness with repulsion . . . for life may be hated or wearied of, but never despised."

Delirious: "Tell me, my neighbor, Mrs. Mays, the pictures never lived, but what of the flowers? Tell them who ask: no rabbis, no ministers, no priests, no speeches, no ceremonies: ah, false—let the living comfort themselves. Tell Sammy's boy, he who flies, tell him to go to Stuttgart and see where Davy has no grave. And what? . . . And what? where millions have no graves—save air."

In delirium or not, wanting the radio on; not seeming to listen, the words still jetting, wanting the music on. Once, silencing it abruptly as of old, she began to cry, unconcealed tears this time. "You have pain, Granny?" Jeannie asked.

"The music," she said, "still it is there and we do not hear; knocks, and our poor human ears too weak. What else, what else we do not hear?"

Once she knocked his hand aside as he gave her a pill, swept the bottles from her bedside table: "no pills, let me feel what I feel," and laughed as on his hands and knees he groped to pick them up.

Nighttimes her hand reached across the bed to hold his.

A constant retching began. Her breath was too faint for sustained speech now, but still the lips moved:

When no longer necessary   to injure others
Pick   pick pick   Blind chicken
As a human being   responsibility

"David!" imperious, "Basin!" and she would vomit, rinse her mouth, the wasted throat working to swallow, and begin the chant again.

She will be better off in the hospital now, the doctor said.

He sent the telegrams to the children, was packing her suitcase, when her hoarse voice startled. She had roused, was pulling herself to sitting.

"Where now?" she asked. "Where now do you drag me?"

"You do not even have to have a baby to go this time," he soothed, looking for the brush to pack. "Remember, after Davy you told me—worthy to have a baby for the pleasure of the ten-day rest in the hospital?"

"Where now? Not home yet?" Her voice mourned. "Where *is* my home?"

He rose to ease her back. "The doctor, the hospital," he started to explain, but deftly, like a snake, she had slithered out of bed and stood swaying, propped behind the night table.

"Coward," she hissed, "runner."

"You stand," he said senselessly.

"To take me there and run. Afraid of a little vomit."

He reached her as she fell. She struggled against him, half slipped from his arms, pulled herself up again.

"Weakling," she taunted, "to leave me there and run. Betrayer. All your life you have run."

He sobbed, telling Jeannie. "A Marilyn Monroe to run for her virtue. Fifty-nine pounds she weighs, the doctor said, and she beats at me like a Dempsey. Betrayer, she cries, and I running like a dog when she calls; day and night, running to her, her vomit, the bedpan. . . ."

"She needs you, Grandaddy," said Jeannie. "Isn't that what they call love? I'll see if she sleeps, and if she does, poor worn-out darling, we'll have a party, you and I: I brought us rum babas."

They did not move her. By her bed now stood the tall hooked pillar that held the solutions—blood and dextrose—to feed her veins. Jeannie moved down the hall to take over the sickroom, her face so radiant, her grandfather asked her once: "you are in love?" (Shameful the joy, the pure overwhelming joy from being with her grandmother; the peace, the serenity that breathed.)

"My darling escape," she answered incoherently, "my darling Granny" —as if that explained.

Now one by one the children came, those that were able. Hannah, Paul, Sammy. Too late to ask: and what did you learn with your living, Mother, and what do we need to know?

Clara, the eldest, clenched:

Pay me back, Mother, pay me back for all you took from me. Those others you crowded into your heart. The hands I needed to be for you, the heaviness, the responsibility.

Is this she? Noises the dying make, the crablike hands crawling over the covers. The ethereal singing.

She hears that music, that singing from childhood; forgotten sound—not heard since, since. . . . And the hardness breaks like a cry: Where did we lose each other, first mother, singing mother?

Annulled: the quarrels, the gibing, the harshness between; the fall into silence and the withdrawal.

I do not know you, Mother. Mother, I never knew you.

Lennie, suffering not alone for her who was dying, but for that in her which never lived (for that which in him might never come to live. From him too, unspoken words: *good-bye Mother who taught me to mother myself.*

Not Vivi, who must stay with her children; not Davy, but he is already here, having to die again with *her* this time, for the living take their dead with them when they die.

Light she grew, like a bird, and, like a bird, sound bubbled in her throat while the body fluttered in agony. Night and day, asleep or awake (though indeed there was no difference now) the songs and the phrases leaping.

And he, who had once dreaded a long dying (from fear of himself, from horror of the dwindling money) now desired her quick death profoundly, for *her* sake. He no longer went out, except when Jeannie forced him to; no longer laughed, except when, in the bright kitchenette, Jeannie coaxed his laughter (and she, who seemed to hear nothing else, would laugh too, conspiratorial wisps of laughter).

Light, like a bird, the fluttering body, the little claw hands, the beaked shadow on her face; and the throat, bubbling, straining.

He tried not to listen, as he tried not to look on the face in which only the forehead remained familiar, but trapped with her the long nights in that little room, the sounds worked themselves into his consciousness, with their punctuation of death swallows, whimpers, gurglings.

Even in reality (swallow) *life's lack of it*
Slaveships   deathtrains   clubs   eeenough
The bell   summon what enables
78,000 in one minute (whisper of a scream) *78,000 human beings   we'll destroy ourselves?*

"Aah, Mrs. Miserable," he said, as if she could hear, "all your life working, and now in bed you lie, servants to tend, you do not even need to call to be tended, and still you work. Such hard work it is to die? Such hard work?"

The body threshed, her hand clung in his. A melody, ghost-thin, hovered on her lips, and like a guilty ghost, the vision of her bent in listening to it, silencing the record instantly he was near. Now, heedless of his presence, she floated the melody on and on.

"Hid it from me," he complained, "how many times you listened to remember it so?" And tried to think when she had first played it, or first begun to silence her few records when he came near—but could reconstruct nothing. There was only this room with its tall hooked pillar and its swarm of sounds.

No man one   except through others
Strong   with the not yet   in the now
Dogma dead   war dead   one country

"It helps, Mrs. Philosopher, words from books? It helps?" And it seemed to him that for seventy years she had hidden a tape recorder, infinitely microscopic, within her, that it had coiled infinite mile on mile, trapping every song, every melody, every word read, heard, and spoken—and that maliciously she was playing back only what said nothing of him, of the children, of their intimate life together.

"Left us indeed, Mrs. Babbler," he reproached, "you who called others babbler and cunningly saved your words. A lifetime you tended and loved, and now not a word of us, for us. Left us indeed? Left me."

And he took out his solitaire deck, shuffled the cards loudly, slapped them down.

Lift high   banner of reason (tatter of an orator's voice)
justice   freedom   light
Humankind   life worthy   capacities
Seeks (blur of shudder) *belong   human being*

"Words, words," he accused, "and what human beings did *you* seek around you, Mrs. Live Alone, and what humankind think worthy?"

Though even as he spoke, he remembered she had not always been isolated, had not always wanted to be alone (as he knew there had been a voice before this gossamer one; before the hoarse voice that broke from silence to lash, make incidents, shame him—a girl's voice of eloquence that spoke their holiest dreams). But again he could reconstruct, image, nothing of what had been before, or when, or how, it had changed.

Ace, queen, jack. The pillar shadow fell, so, in two tracks; in the mirror depths glistened a moonlike blob, the empty solution bottle. And it worked in him: *of reason and justice and freedom . . . Dogma dead*: he remembered the full quotation, laughed bitterly. "Hah, good you do not know what you say; good Victor Hugo died and did not see it, his twentieth century."

Deuce, ten, five. Dauntlessly she began a song of their youth of belief:

These things shall be, a loftier race
than e'er the world hath known shall rise
with flame of freedom in their souls
and light of knowledge in their eyes
King, four, jack "In the twentieth century, hah!"

They shall be gentle, brave and strong
to spill no drop of blood, but dare
all . . .
    on earth and fire and sea and air

"To spill no drop of blood, hah! So, cadaver, and you too, cadaver Hugo, 'in the twentieth century ignorance will be dead, dogma will be dead, war will be dead, and for all mankind one country—of fulfilment?' Hah!"

And every life (long strangling cough) *shall*
    be a song

The cards fell from his fingers. Without warning, the bereavement and betrayal he had sheltered—compounded through the years—hidden even from himself—revealed itself,
uncoiled
released,
sprung

and with it the monstrous shapes of what had actually happened in the century.

A ravening hunger or thirst seized him. He groped into the kitchenette, switched on all three lights, piled a tray—"you have finished your night snack, Mrs. Cadaver, now I will have mine." And he was shocked at the tears that splashed on the tray.

"Salt tears. For free. I forgot to shake on salt?"

Whispered: "Lost, how much I lost."

Escaped to the grandchildren whose childhoods were childish, who had never hungered, who lived unravaged by disease in warm houses of many rooms, had all the school for which they cared, could walk on any street, stood a head taller than their grandparents, towered above—beautiful skins, straight backs, clear straightforward eyes. "Yes, you in Olshana," he said to the town of sixty years ago, "they would seem nobility to you."

And was this not the dream then, come true in ways undreamed? he asked.

And are there no other children in the world? he answered, as if in her harsh voice.

And the flame of freedom, the light of knowledge?
And the drop, to spill no drop of blood?

And he thought that at six Jeannie would get up and it would be his turn to go to her room and sleep, that he could press the buzzer and she would come now; that in the afternoon Ellen Mays was coming, and this time they would play cards and he could marvel at how rouge can stand half an inch on the cheek; that in the evening the doctor would come, and he could beg him to be merciful, to stop the feeding solutions, to let her die.

To let her die, and with her their youth of belief out of which her bright, betrayed words foamed; stained words, that on her working lips came stainless.

Hours yet before Jeannie's turn. He could press the buzzer and wake her to come now; he could take a pill, and with it sleep; he could pour more brandy into his milk glass, though what he had poured was not yet touched.

Instead he went back, checked her pulse, gently tended with his knotty fingers as Jeannie had taught.

She was whimpering; her hand crawled across the covers for his. Compassionately he enfolded it, and with his free hand gathered up the cards again. Still was there thirst or hunger ravening in him.

That world of their youth—dark, ignorant, terrible with hate and disease—how was it that living in it, in the midst of corruption, filth, treachery, degradation, they had not mistrusted man nor themselves; had believed so beautifully, so . . . falsely?

"Aaah, children," he said out loud, "how we believed, how we belonged." And he yearned to package for each of the children, the grandchildren, for everyone, *that joyous certainty, that sense of mattering, of moving and being moved, of being one and indivisible with the great of the past, with all that freed, ennobled.* Package it, stand on corners, in front of stadiums and on crowded beaches, knock on doors, give it as a fabled gift.

"And why not in cereal boxes, in soap packages?" he mocked himself. "Aah. You have taken my senses, cadaver."

Words foamed, died unsounded. Her body writhed; she made kissing motions with her mouth. (Her lips moving as she read, poring over the Book of the Martyrs, the magnifying glass superimposed over the heavy eyeglasses.) *Still she believed?* "Eva!" he whispered. "Still you believed? You lived by it? These Things Shall Be?"

"One pound soup meat," she answered distinctly, "one soup bone."

"My ears heard you. Ellen Mays was witness: 'Humankind . . . one has to believe.'" Imploringly: "Eva!"

"Bread, day-old." She was mumbling. "Please, in a wooden box . . . for kindling. The thread, hah, the thread breaks. Cheap thread"—and a gurgling, enormously loud, began in her throat.

"I ask for stone; she gives me bread—day-old." He pulled his hand away, shouted: "Who wanted questions? Everything you have to wake?" Then dully, "Ah, let me help you turn, poor creature."

Words jumbled, cleared. In a voice of crowded terror:

"Paul, Sammy, don't fight.

"Hannah, have I ten hands?

"How can I give it, Clara, how can I give it if I don't have?"

"You lie," he said sturdily, "there was joy too." Bitterly: "Ah how cheap you speak of us at the last."

As if to rebuke him, as if her voice had no relationship with her flailing body, she sang clearly, beautifully, a school song the children had taught her when they were little; begged:

"Not look   my hair   where they cut. . . ."

(The crown of braids shorn.) And instantly he left the mute old woman poring over the Book of the Martyrs; went past the mother treading at the sewing machine, singing with the children; past the girl in her wrinkled prison dress, hiding her hair with scarred hands, lifting to him her awkward, shamed, imploring eyes of love; and took her in his arms, dear, personal, fleshed, in all the heavy passion he had loved to rouse from her.

"Eva!"

Her little claw hand beat the covers. How much, how much can a man stand? He took up the cards, put them down, circled the beds, walked to the dresser, opened, shut drawers, brushed his hair, moved his hand bit by bit over the mirror to see what of the reflection he could blot out with each move, and felt that at any moment he would die of what was unendurable. Went to press the buzzer to wake Jeannie, looked down, saw on Jeannie's sketch pad the hospital bed, with *her;* the double bed alongside, with him; the tall pillar feeding into her veins, and their hands, his and hers, clasped, feeding each other. And as if he had been instructed he went to his bed, lay down, holding the sketch (as if it could shield against the monstrous shapes of loss, of betrayal, of death) and with his free hand took hers back into his.

So Jeannie found them in the morning.

That last day the agony was perpetual. Time after time it lifted her almost off the bed, so they had to fight to hold her down. He could not endure and left the room; wept as if there never would be tears enough.

Jeannie came to comfort him. In her light voice she said: Grandaddy, Grandaddy don't cry. She is not there, she promised me. On the last day, she said she would go back to when she first heard music, a little girl on the road of the village where she was born. She promised me. It is a wedding and they dance, while the flutes so joyous and vibrant tremble in the air. Leave her there, Grandaddy, it is all right. She promised me. Come back, come back and help her poor body to die.